Home School:

Where

Learning

Is

For Life

By

Jacqueline Olivia Cross

ISBN: 978-1-4107-4259-9 (sc)
ISBN: 978-1-4107-4258-2 (e)

Library of Congress Control Number: 2003093259

Print information available on the last page.

This book is printed on acid-free paper.

1stBooks - rev. 09/03/2020

Dedication

This book and my life are dedicated to my Abba Father. To fully express my gratitude would require the writing of another book. Let me simply say "Thank you Lord!"

I also dedicate this book to my husband, my very best friend, Michael Anthony Cross. You are the most patient man in the world (on most days). I most humbly say "Thank you dear."

To my children, Michael, Mark, Jennifer, Janet, Matthew & Micah, who taught me more than I could have ever imagined, I say "Thank you. I love you and pray God's blessing upon your earthly endeavors."

To my Mother and Father, Charles and Lillian Ware, I say "I love you more than words can express! Thank you for teaching me through your life a sacrificial kind of love!"

To my longtime friends, Bob and Emilie Barnes, "Thank you for teaching me home organization techniques! Without these tools, home schooling would have been impossible for us.

Charles and Lillian Ware

About the Book

Home School: Where Learning Is For Life takes the reader through twenty years of the Cross family's home schooling adventure, but it doesn't end there. It is crammed full of wisdom learned by trial and error, both from other families and many years of their wonderful experiences. It is packed with helpful information and practical tips that can be used for many years to come. Most importantly, it walks the reader through their spiritual journey. Each chapter begins with a verse specifically chosen to lead the reader home.

Home School: Where Learning Is For Life is a book of hope and encouragement from beginning to end. It was written to serve families, especially mothers in the home who are looking for help and confirmation that they're on the right path.

Home School: Where Learning Is For Life is an answer to the call of God to "feed my sheep." At a time in our nation's history when the definitions of God, human being, family, male, female are being redefined, here is a book about simple belief, unfaltering faith and obedience.

What are other authors saying about Home School: Where Learning Is For Life?

"I laughed, I cried, I identified. This book doesn't sugar coat or see home schooling through rose colored glasses but it honestly challenges, encourages and reflects the heart of a woman of God." *Sue Cutting is author of Chaos Under Control-A Guide to Home Organization*

"What a pleasure to read such godly material. This shouldn't just be for home schoolers, but for all families. You truly have captured the spirit of Christian marriage and family. Tears came to our eyes as we reviewed all of your thoughts. What a great chronological history of your family's life. Our prayers will be that your material will be spread throughout the Christian community. You have certainly raised the bar when it comes to raising children. Oh, if every parent had your zeal for truth and the desire to model a godly home." *Bob & Emilie Barnes are co-authors of numerous books on home management & marriage-More Hours in My Day, Creative Home Organizer, Growing a Great Marriage. Two of their latest books are, Strength for Today, Bright Hope for Tomorrow and Join Me For Tea.*

"Home School: Where Learning Is For Life is an invaluable resource of encouragement and hope to home schoolers who are in it for the long haul. You will be touched, inspired and spurred on by the Cross family's personal testimony. I have had to the joy of training Jacqueline at CLASS." *Florence Littauer is a gifted author best known for her books Personality Plus and Silver Boxes. Her newest titles are Personality Plus for Couples and Personality Plus for Parents. She is a speaker and teacher with CLASServices, Inc.*

Table of Contents

Introduction

"My purpose is that they may be encouraged in heart
and unified in love, so that they may have the full riches of
complete understanding, in order that they may know
the mystery of God, namely Christ, in whom are hidden all
the treasures of wisdom and knowledge."
Colossians 2:2,3

I wanted to write a simple book. I wanted to write a book that Mom could sit down with a cup of tea and read, like a visit with a friend. I wanted to write a book that Dad wouldn't mind skimming through. I wanted to write a book that reflected our family's home schooling journey and to share our experiences. I wanted to write a book that only someone with years of home schooling experience could provide. I make no claim to fame. I exalt no degree. I am plain and simply a mother. I am Michael's helpmate, friend, and the mother of six children, Michael, Mark, Jennifer, Janet, Matthew, and Micah. I am a daughter of the King! We (my husband Michael and I) wanted to give parents hope and encouragement from beginning to end.

When you read this book, remember that it is written primarily from the heart, not from the grammarian perspective. Jacqueline (jc Galatians 2:20) is primarily the author, but every page was read and tweaked by Michael and the children for details. We do not present this book or ourselves as people who have arrived. We have made our share of mistakes, but we have also done some things right. We have washed many loads of laundry, cried many a tear, cleaned many a mess, refereed many an argument and prayed many a prayer. We have asked the same questions that you are probably asking like, "What curriculum are you using and how long does it take you to home school?" Or "How do you clean the house, nurse a baby and teach the toddlers or an older child?" We have been there, done that and ordered the t-shirts to boot! We wish we had tallied up the mileage on the car used to drive to all of the different homes, parks, field trips, academic endeavors and sports events. And to think, it is not over for us yet.

> "What curriculum are you using and how long does it take you to home school?" Or "How do you clean the house, nurse a baby, and teach the toddlers or an older child?"

Today, the oldest of our six children, Michael Christopher (22), is working for an insurance company and going to school in Texas. Our second son, Mark Anthony (21) is in college. Our twin daughters, Jennifer and Janet (18) graduated from our home school this past June. They completed high school during their two years at the local community college and are now attending a local university. Our fourth son, Matthew (13), is being home schooled again after attending a charter school for special needs children last year. Our youngest son Micah Andrew (10) is home schooling us.

Our family started its home schooling adventure the day our children were born, but officially in 1982. Curriculum choices were simple then and home schooling was not quite so popular. Home schooling has grown by leaps and bounds these last few years. According to current statistics our numbers are estimated to be in the millions. It is very obvious to those of us who have home schooled for a while that home schooling has become a huge marketplace.

We have attended many state home school conventions over that last eighteen years in Virginia, Delaware and Ohio. While it is a blessing to have so many choices offered at these convention halls, I fear for those just starting out in home schooling because home schooling has become a maze of educational and religious philosophies and products.

I recall an incident a few years ago at the CHEO (Christian Home Educators of Ohio) convention in Columbus. I had just completed another of the excellent sessions provided when I made a quick dash for the convention. I stood almost paralyzed for a second looking up and down the vendor aisles. I felt as if an overwhelming oppressive cloud was over me as I stood there trying to decide which way to go first. "What confusion!" I thought. "How must a brand new home schooler feel?" I came to the convention with a plan and knew exactly what I wanted to buy and which sessions I wanted to attend. Yet, even as a veteran home schooler, I still felt overwhelmed! It was then that the Lord planted a seed of compassion to write this book for those home schoolers just starting out or any home schooler who felt lost in the maze of philosophies and products.

Our prayer for you is that your family would find help and encouragement in this book. We pray that your family would come to know God more deeply, trust Him more fully and lean on Him completely to meet all of your home schooling needs.

What God did for us, He can do for your family too. He met all of our needs along the way. We began our home schooling adventure in 1982 while we were living in Victorville, California. My husband, Michael, was a young lieutenant in the Air Force stationed at George, AFB. We were struggling in our young marriage and had just been introduced to Christ. The idea of a personal relationship with a living God was a new concept for us. Michael had been raised in the Catholic faith and I in the Methodist church (African Methodist Episcopal).

After four years in Victorville, we were transferred to a base in Las Vegas. "Sin City!" we thought. But Las Vegas was actually the place where we really began to grow as Christians. God provided the spiritual support we needed in many ways. We discovered a great Christian radio station where we daily heard the Word and learned of various church opportunities in the area. He provided us with great neighbors with whom we interacted, who each had spiritual pilgrimages of their own. He provided a wonderful pastor and body of believers. He provided a local home school support group named Home Schools United-Vegas Valley for our young family.

This first support group was made up of one hundred families of various religious and non-religious backgrounds. I sensed a call to prepare myself for possible service to home schoolers should I ever need to start a group when we transferred again. Michael and I joined the board of Home Schools United-Vegas Valley. We gained more than we gave. We learned so much by interacting with the different families.

We learned that some families used old, outdated textbooks given away by the public schools. Some families could not afford to purchase the expensive catalog curriculum. Other families used outdated curriculum sold by the local Christian school to save money. Some chose to contact publishers directly and arrange their own curriculum. Then there were those who used a child-directed approach, utilizing the interest of the child to guide their studies.

They took full advantage of home educating and made extensive use of the library. We met and witnessed families successfully educating and graduating their children through home education in 1987.

> *We gained more than we gave. We learned so much by interacting with the different families.*

By the time we transferred to Virginia in the summer of 1988, I was excited to learn of several support groups in the area. Unfortunately, most were formed around churches and outsiders weren't encouraged to join. Since the local church we attended already had three home schooling families, the Lord led me to start a group. Our little group soon grew to seventeen families. For several years, both children and adults grew in our friendships and understanding of home educating. We took field trips together. We studied art and music together. We lifted up and encouraged one another. And, we prayed together.

Then, it was time to move again. Michael was transferred to Wright Patterson AFB in Ohio. After five years in a Virginia rental house that did not allow pets and a yard that had no space to plant a garden, we yearned for open space and animals. We wanted freedom from the public school schedule that a suburban neighborhood imposed. We purchased a five-acre mini-farm in the country just outside of Xenia, Ohio. We were delighted and thankful to discover a group of sixty home schooling families in that area. That was nine years ago and since that time, the number of families has tripled.

This book grew out of a need to encourage other mothers in our PEACH (Parents Educating At Christian Homes) support group. God seems to be adding daily to those who are beginning to home school. During my early years as a Christian and a home educator, I desired for an older, more experienced woman to take me under her wings and teach me. But I never found her. In my study of Titus 2:3-5, God convicted my heart to become one. As a couple, we could have benefited so much from the mentoring of an older wiser couple. May the Lord convict your hearts to become one...

Home Schools – Vegas Valley

Parents Educating At Christian Homes

A Parent's Prayer

"O God, make me a better parent."

Help me to understand my children, to listen patiently to what they have to say and to answer all their questions kindly. Keep me from interrupting them, talking back to them and contradicting them. Make me as courteous to them as I would have them be to me. Give me the courage to confess my sins against my children and to ask of them forgiveness, when I know I have done them wrong.

May I not vainly hurt the feelings of my children. Forbid that I should laugh at their mistakes or resort to shame and ridicule as punishment. Let me not tempt a child to lie or steal. So guide me hour by hour that I may demonstrate by all I say and do that honesty produces happiness. Reduce, I pray, the meanness in me. May I cease to nag: and when I am out of sorts, help me, Oh Lord, to hold my tongue.

Blind me to the little errors of my children and help me see the good things that they do. Give me a ready word for honest praise.

Help me to treat my children as those of their own age, but let me not exact of them the judgments and conventions of adults. Allow me not to rob them of the opportunity to wait upon themselves, to think, to choose and to make decisions.

Forbid that I should ever punish them for any selfish satisfaction. May I grant them all of their wishes that are reasonable and have the courage always to withhold a privilege which I know will do them harm.

Make me so fair and just, so considerate and companionable to my children that they will have a genuine esteem for me. Fit me to be loved and imitated by my children.
With all thy gifts, Oh God, do give me calm and poise and self-control.

છ્ય છ્ય છ્ય

By Garry Cleveland Myers, PH.D.

Co-Founder of Highlights For Children

Copyright 1969,1994

Highlights For Children, Inc., Columbus, Ohio

Part One

The Early Years of Home Educating

Chapter 1

Where Do I Begin?

"So God created man in His own image,
In the image of God he created him,
Male and female he created them."
Genesis 1:27

I lay on the hospital bed, pregnant and in intense pain. My husband Michael left the room to find a nurse. I was all alone, struggling to focus in the La Maze breathing technique I had been taught. All the breathing may have helped me to get my mind off of my suffering with our first child, but it simply wasn't working with our second. So I decided to throw out the La Maze breathing and I began to pray. My thoughts went back to the beginning. All the way back to Genesis. "Lord," I prayed, "I know that I'm suffering because of the curse. I know Eve sinned and now we women bring forth children in pain. Please forgive me for my sins, please help me…" My prayer trailed on and it wasn't long before I was getting the urge to push. There was no husband, nurse or doctor in the room to say "No, don't push," so I did what came naturally.

Suddenly, the door flew open and I heard the nurse yell for an airman to come into the room. Our second son Mark plopped onto the bed and was scooped immediately into the hands of the airman to be suctioned and wiped off. I lay there feeling good. It felt wonderful to be able to do what God had designed me to do, to procreate.

Taking the La Maze class and reading the books could not have fully prepared me for what lay ahead. Only experiencing birth truly gave meaning to the words. Then we learned a new word: teamwork. My husband Michael found himself juggling his responsibilities. He was a navigator on the Phantom F-4 with duties as an Electronic Warfare officer. His job required finding surface to air missiles and destroying them. He was flying all over the place. Now added to the mix, were mom (me) and the new baby Mark at the hospital while Grandma Audrey stayed home with one year old Michael Christopher.

It wasn't long before my husband Michael was back on the job and my life was full with loving babies, nursing, laundry, cooking and cleaning. Within the next few months, a Christian family named the McGreers introduced us to Christ and home schooling. We noticed that Chris and Nancy took their children out of a Christian school to home school and we could not understand why. "Aren't we called to be salt and light?" I asked one day.

Nancy invited me to come and observe her home school one day. She gave me a book to read by Dr. Raymond Moore called <u>Home Grown Kids</u>. It told of exposing the children to diseases and peer pressure at such young ages and many other things that I had not thought about. The seed was planted. I shared it with my husband Michael and we both agreed with many of Dr. Moore's points; they made good sense. The book opened my mind to the realization that I was going to have to take a more active part than packing a lunch, putting them on a school bus and kissing them goodbye.

> ### *Aren't we called to be salt and light?*
> ### *I asked one day.*

In the fall of 1984, we moved into a small Las Vegas neighborhood. At that time, Michael Christopher was four, Mark was three and our twin babies Jennifer and Janet were nine months old. I watched as several of the young mothers with pre-schoolers raced to get them enrolled in either public or private school programs. I watched as they struggled to get breakfast down them, tossed babies into car seats, and raced back and forth for the two-hour pre-school programs. I also saw the construction paper projects that came home. I observed the results of financial strain and stressed marriages.

While the other mothers raced off to programs, I taught my children Bible stories, how to sort laundry, how to make beds, and how to clean their rooms. I had attended a seminar called More Hours in My Day on home management taught by Emilie Barnes. I incorporated many of her ideas plus my own in teaching and training the children. We made construction paper projects together. They helped in the kitchen. They made messes in the kitchen. They spent many hours enjoying outdoor play, building, creating and wrecking. When I went shopping, they were there with me, learning to compare prices, brands, use coupons, meet people and pay for the groceries. They traveled with me to the Post office, the cleaners, the dentist, and the park. Though extremely difficult to travel with babies and toddlers, each outing we took was an opportunity to teach and to train. We were home schooling.

Our trip to the lake

Chapter 2

Why Home School?

"For the message of the cross is foolishness to those who are perishing,
But to us who are being saved it is the power of God.
For it is written: I will destroy the wisdom of the wise;
The intelligence of the intelligent I will frustrate.
Where is the wise man? Where is the scholar?
Where is the philosopher of this age?
Has not God made foolish the wisdom of the world?"
I Corinthians 1:18

Michael pulled our 1984 blue mini-van along side the curb in front of the base chapel at Nellis Air Force Base. Just as I slid the side door open, a friendly woman passing by came over to greet us. "Hi! I'm Sharon one of the chaplain's wives." "Hi!" I returned the greeting as I unloaded the last of our four children. "I hear you're a home schooler," Sharon said as she looked down at the young ages of the children. "Yes," I replied. Somehow the look on her face spoke volumes. I took it as a disapproval of what we were attempting to do: home educate.

"I'm going to be teaching in a local Christian school," Sharon said. Michael, now having parked the car, came up just in time for us to ask her a few questions about education in general. (We had been doing this for months, asking anyone who said they were a teacher about their educational experiences.) She shared her knowledge and we shared what we learned from the book Home Grown Kids by Dr. Raymond Moore concerning children being exposed to communicable diseases, peer pressure and rushed academics.

A few months later, Sharon's children began to have trouble in their classrooms at the Christian school in which she taught. She thought that being a Christian and a teacher would help her to better communicate and resolve the issue with her daughter's teacher. But it didn't work out as she planned. I loaned her a copy of Dr. Moore's book. By this time, her husband had been sent away on temporary duty assignment for several months and she mailed a copy of the book to him. They decided to home school the following year.

In my neighborhood, all the young mothers were putting their six-year-olds in school full time. "I don't understand," a neighbor confided as we stood in my front yard one afternoon, "How can my daughter be failing first grade in her second month of school?" she asked looking at me in a puzzling way. "What do you mean?" I countered, realizing her obvious distress. "Her teacher sent this card home saying that because she can't read, she is going to be put in this special group." "A special group?" I repeated. "Shannon knows that means the dummies," her mother said, "I thought they went to first grade to learn their alphabets, numbers and then to read." She shook her head in disbelief and turned to go back up the street to her home, while I stood there logging this conversation in the back of my mind. There always seemed to be this nagging question in my mind. "Was home schooling doing the right thing or the best thing for my children?"

A few weeks later, another neighbor with a six-year-old son in the local public school shared her observations about her volunteer time in her son's class. She was becoming more and more agitated after each week of volunteering. "If parents knew the way their children were behaving, they wouldn't have their children in there." She home schooled the following year.

> ## "Was home schooling doing the right thing or the best thing for my children?"

Our son Michael Christopher was now six and we had definitely decided to home school. Our faith was growing, as was our desire to share this newfound love of Jesus. The more scripture we read, the more convinced we became that our children were our first disciples. We clearly saw that if we gained the whole world yet lost our children then we would have failed as parents.

Home schooling allowed us to make the Bible foundational to our children's education. Daily we could incorporate our studies in the Word into real life examples. We taught them about our Heavenly Father – about His plan to save mankind through His son Jesus. We taught this through everyday life and experiences. We didn't understand it all; we simply walked by faith. In later years, we came to a better understanding of the work of the Holy Spirit in our lives.

Home schooling allowed us to slow the fast pace of life. It eliminated the need to drive back and forth to school each day. It eliminated the need to buy large quantities of school clothes. We were then able to use that money as an investment in the lives of our children for the purchase of curriculum and materials that we felt important and necessary for their growth and maturity.

Home schooling allowed us flexibility. We were able to capitalize on the children's excitement about learning and utilize teachable moments in their lives as opposed to page after page in a workbook. We visited the newspaper print room, the bank, the police station, the museum and the library. Occasionally we took trips with Dad.

Home schooling allowed us to feed our children nutritious food. It allowed us to eliminate the memorization of unnecessary information. It allowed us to discover their spiritual gifts. It allowed us to protect their minds from evil. It allowed us to teach them to discern. It allowed us to teach them self-control and self-motivation.

> *"Home schooling allowed us to make the Bible foundational to our children's education."*

We discovered as a family that we were each unique individuals created by God and each endowed with different gifts and abilities. We discovered that our family was building strong relationships. The children were becoming friends with each other. At times they were the worst of enemies. Eventually, they learned to support, encourage and correct one another. As they grew, we began to see each other's spiritual gifts and appreciate our differences.

I suppose if you asked one hundred families why they chose to home educate, you would probably get one hundred different reasons. Some folks have had bad experiences with teachers in both public and private schools. Others have had peer problems, curriculum problems, or their own child's inability to adapt to the traditional school setting. Some could not afford the cost of a private school education. Then, there are some like our family who believe God called us to home school.

The Cross Family

1981

Chapter 3

Discovering Yourself as the Teacher

"Hear, O Israel: The Lord our God, the Lord is one.
Love the Lord your God with all your heart and with all your soul
And with all your strength.
These commandments that I give you today are to be upon your hearts.
Impress them on your children. Talk about them when you sit at home and when you walk along
The road, when you lie down and when you get up. Tie them as symbols on your hands and bind
Them on your foreheads. Write them on the doorframes of your houses and on your gates."
Deuteronomy 6:4-9

I walked into the kitchen when I heard all of the commotion six-year-old Michael and five-year-old Mark were making. "It's mine!" one shouted. "No, it's mine!" another cried. They yanked the heavy wooden barstool back and forth. I stood there for a few seconds trying to figure out just how I should approach the situation. "Give me wisdom Lord," I muttered as I headed for the boys.

The day before, our Bible lesson was about the wisdom of King Solomon. The Lord gave me an idea. "What's the matter boys?" I asked. "I got the stool first!" they stated emphatically and almost in unison. "No you didn't! It's mine!" and the tug of war began again. "Boys! Boys! I smiled "You don't have to fight over this one stool. Look, we have two." Neither one was interested in the other stool. "O.K.!" I said, "I've got an idea and I disappeared into the garage. I reappeared with the saw. The teeth of the saw must have looked shark-like because their eyes grew as big as saucers. "Remember the story we read yesterday about the two women fighting over the baby? I asked. "Well, let's cut the stool in half and I'll give half to each of you. "No!" the pleaded and began to work out a deal between themselves. "Wow!" I thought, "King Solomon's wisdom really worked," and I returned the saw to its' place in the garage.

That incident opened my eyes to the fact that I was a teacher. Did I know enough? Did I need to be a certified teacher with a Bachelor or Master's Degree? Would a high school diploma be enough? Did I have the patience? Would I merely duplicate the way I had learned? All of these were questions that entered my mind over time.

That summer, I decided to volunteer to teach in a two-week session of Vacation Bible School at College Park Baptist Church in Las Vegas. Ironically, my helper was a first grade teacher in one of the local public schools. We became very well acquainted during that time and she discussed many of her experiences with teaching. She spoke of the difficulty of teaching due to all the problems she encountered in school. "I can't even begin to teach," she said, "when some of these children aren't mentally ready to learn. Mom is dropping them off at the sitter's so early that by the time they get to school, they are too tired or too hungry to learn." "Some of the children," she said, "come from abusive homes and some are from single parent homes." On and on she went telling me of her experiences in the classroom. She offered to test Michael my six-year-old in her home. I was both relieved and pleased with the results. Though never having been in school, he was already testing well above his grade level.

Sarah, another first grade teacher in our church, shared her experiences with me. "I'm frustrated," she said to me one day. "In my school building, I work in a room that has no windows. I went to the principal to ask if I could go outside to read a book to my students and she told me "No." It was so pretty outside. All I wanted was to have the green trees and grass around me and my students as I read to them about nature and butterflies."

I felt sad for Sarah and her students. Here these children were at an age to enjoy the beauty of God's earth and they were being forced to accept it all from a book. Later, Sarah shared several stacks of her old worksheets with me. The next day my children and I used some of them. As we worked on the pages, I looked out of the windows to see a butterfly. "*Why did I feel so tied to a worksheet when God so richly provided nature all around us,*" I thought. I stopped what we were doing and took our children into the back yard. We lay in the grass. We looked up at the tall cottonwood trees as the luscious green leaves danced happily in the wind. We watched the clouds floating by. We watched the butterflies. We thanked God for the beauty all around us and for the privilege to home educate. Home schooling gave us the freedom to use the world God created to bring many lessons to life.

> ### *Did I know enough? Did I need to be a certified teacher with a Bachelor or Master's Degree? Would a high school diploma be enough?*

As time passed, Michael and I were gaining confidence in our abilities to home educate. We had been primary care givers for our babies as they nursed, crawled, walked, were potty trained, used a cup, ate solid food, sang their ABC's and Jesus Loves Me song. We taught them how to speak English. Why now were we too ignorant to teach them? Hadn't we completed twelve years of education and beyond?

The question to ask is not "Am I qualified to teach my children?" rather the questions should be, "Am I willing to obey God? Am I willing to teach my children and their children after them the praiseworthy deeds of the Lord? Am I willing to teach them to 'Love the Lord their God with all their hearts and with all their soul and with all their strength?' Am I willing to impress the commands of the Lord on their hearts? Am I willing to talk about these commands at home and when we walk along the road, when we lie down and when we get up? Am I willing to sacrifice for a season in my children's lives? Do I have a teachable spirit? Am I willing to learn, change and be a living example for my children to emulate?"

Over the years, I have met many home schooling parents. The mothers tend to be the primary teachers. Some of these women have had degrees and some have home schooled without college degrees. I have noticed that those with teaching degrees consistently state that having a degree in education has not given them any significant advantage when it came to home schooling their own children. They still had to take the time to discover their child. A few have confessed that they had to throw out some of their educational theories learned in college. You can do it! You can home school with a degree or without.

> ### *"Am I willing to obey God? ...Do I have a teachable spirit? Am I willing to learn, change and be a living example for my children to emulate?"*

If you have a personal relationship with Jesus Christ, then you have the Holy Spirit dwelling in you. He is the ultimate teacher and guide. You as parents are simply the earthen vessels through whom He does His work to grow the children to maturity in Christ and to become responsible adults. *If you are not sure how to have a personal relationship with Jesus, send for a personalized copy of our testimony in a booklet called <u>The Witness Booklet</u>. (See address in the back of this book)

Michael and Mark at Work and at Play

Chapter 4

Discovering Your Child as the Student

"Train up a child in the way he should go,
And when he is old he will not turn from it."
Proverbs 22:6
"I am convinced that these children come pre-wired and pre-measured,
But with no directions on the package. But thank the Lord for parents, grandparents, sisters, brothers, aunts,
Uncles, friends, neighbors and the Body of Christ. Because…someone, somewhere has
Gone through it before and can give wise counsel."
Jacqueline Olivia Cross

<u>Child #1 Michael Christopher</u>

The phone rang. "Hello, Mrs. Cross?" asked the voice on the other end. "Yes," I answered. "This is Mrs. Johnson, I'm Michael's Sunday school teacher," she said. I recognized the voice before she even finished speaking. "Mrs. Cross," she slowly and hesitantly proceeded, I don't know how to tell you this but I think something is wrong with Michael's eye." She paused. I was listening intently and waiting anxiously for each word. "I'm a nursing student," she said, "we're studying the eye right now and I think you might want to get it checked."

I thanked her for calling, I was grateful that she cared enough to call. I made an appointment with an ophthalmologist. The doctor told me Michael had Anosometrophic Ambylopia, basically a lazy eye. If we had we waited six months to a year longer, he might have lost his sight totally in that eye. Michael would need to be patched for several years. It was also during this time that I was told of special classes for children with special needs available for Michael.

In public, other children were already beginning to ask questions or stare at Michael. He was beginning to feel real "special." "Hey kid! What ya doing with that band-aid on ya eye?" became common. I knew I didn't want Michael to think less of himself or his abilities due to the patch, so we allowed him to work at his own pace and pursue his interests at home. We were thankful that he was a self-motivated student.

Child #2 Mark Anthony

It didn't take long for us to discover that our second child was different from our first. I'll never forget the night we went to pick up my children from the Sunday school room. My husband Michael and I had completed visitations for the Outreach program. The children were taken care of while we parents went to visit those who had visited the church. "Three good and one bad!" the young college student said as she looked directly down at five- year-old Mark. Obviously, his behavior had not been good.

The student's comment made me angry. In fact, I was furious. *There are ways of correcting a child without attacking them personally*, I thought. But I never said a word. I quietly took the children by the hand and led them to our car. "Didn't she realize the power of her words?" I asked myself. I knew that my child behaved differently, and I also knew that he had a strong will. Mark loved to tease.

Our second son, Mark, needed to learn obedience, self-control and a few other things. But these character traits were going to take lots of years to work on and develop. His behavior at the time should not have labeled him as "bad." With our son Mark, there always seemed to be this war of the wills. When my husband Michael and I drew lines in the sand, he crossed them to make sure we meant what we said. Our first child, Michael Christopher, always responded immediately. If we looked at him with displeasure, that was worse than any spanking.

Discovery Zones

At home, we observed our children in their play with us as adults and their interactions with their siblings. We began to notice strengths and weaknesses in their characters and their ability to learn and understand various concepts.

In the neighborhood, we were able to observe their play with other children outside of our family. We utilized the feedback from babysitters, neighbors, friends, aunts, uncles, Sunday school teachers, or grandparents. These were all individuals who provided feedback and aided us in assessing and evaluating our child.

At church, we usually volunteered to assist the teacher or taught the class ourselves. This too, provided great insight into our child as compared with others their age. This comparison is not the negative kind of comparison that belittles them, but the kind of comparison that aids the parent in knowing the child is developing properly.

We also noticed things about our children that reminded us of a grandparent, a brother or a sister and we realized that heredity does play a part also. There were times when we looked into our children's faces and it was as if we were looking into a mirror and seeing a reflection of ourselves.

We knew that our children were unique gifts of God. Each specially designed for His purpose. We eventually learned not to compare them but to accept them as individuals with a learning style and pace of their own. This is a hard thing to do, but as parents, we should strive to train them in the way the Lord made them. We should not force them into a mold to make them socially acceptable or to make them what we want them to be. It is the way God wants them to go that works best. You will find as we did, that once you accept your child the way God created them, you will find peace, love and joy in your relationship. You will love them for who they are and not for how they perform. Therefore, tailor the curriculum to your child, not, your child to the curriculum!

Mark & Michael at play

Chapter 5

What Do You Do With Babies and Toddlers?

"Not by might, nor by power, but by my spirit, saith the Lord of Hosts."
Zechariah 4:6
"From the lips of children and infants you have ordained praise."
Psalm 8:2

L ook at all those arms and legs!" the technician stated as I lay flat on my back with the gooey jelly squirted out all over my abdomen and his instrument moving and circling around. I tried to make out whatever was on the monitor, but I could not. "What do you mean?" I asked, but he said he was not allowed to tell me anything, the doctor would be the one to inform me at my visit. My mind began to fill with panic and joy. "I'm in the twilight zone!" I muttered to myself. I recalled a dream I had several weeks before of giving birth to five babies. Their names were Faith, Hope, Charity and Love. I strained my brain to remember the fifth one but could not. I was relieved and disappointed all at the same time when I heard that I was giving birth to twins.

I began to dilate and contract at 28 weeks, so I was placed on complete bed rest. My blessed mother put her life on hold for three months to live with us and assist with three-year-old Michael and two-year-old Mark. Jennifer Michelle & Janet Marie made their entrance into the world on November 27th, 1983. My life was full of mothering babies. I had a three year old, a two year old and twin babies, four car seats, tons of diapers and a home to manage. I traveled for many months with a newborn in the front pack (Gerry Cuddler) and a newborn in the backpack, a three year old in the right hand and a two year old in my left hand. I must have looked like a mother duck, followed by my ducklings. I know what the baby and toddler years are like and I survived! Michael and I survived by taking one day at a time, by working together, by trusting that the Holy Spirit was really the Teacher and Guide.

I have walked through the valley of the shadow of babies. Yes, I know that sounds terrible but if you've had one child after another you'll understand what I mean. I have spent many years on top of Mount Never-Rest! I have lived through the ear infections, the trips to the emergency room for falls, bronchitis, pneumonia, and asthma. And let's not talk about the piles of laundry, dirty diapers, wet beds, sticky fingers or absolute messes they made. I don't call these years "a valley" because they are terrible years, I call them this because they are difficult years. They are years when the little ones consume all of your time, energy and effort. As Dr. James Dobson says "They are walking emergencies."

> ***"Michael and I survived by taking one day at a time, by working together and by trusting that the Holy Spirit was really the Teacher and Guide."***

I recall one day when the twins were toddlers, they decided to divide and conquer me. We had moved into a new house and been there about a week when one twin went in one direction to pull out all of the items from underneath the kitchen sink, the other went into the bathroom to pull out the items from underneath the bathroom cabinet. Then there were the days when an older child might say "Mommm- mmmee! I don't understand this math problem, will you help me? Or "Mommm-meeee! I don't understand what they mean about a contraction?" Or "Mommm-mmeee! Mommm-meeee! Mommmm-mmmeee!" just kept coming and I wanted to stop everything and simply, "Screammmmmmmmmmmmmmm!!!!!"

How do parents, especially moms hear that still small voice amidst the frustration and chaotic times? I believe before that chaos ever begins, we must seek intimate fellowship with our Creator and the giver of all gifts. We must seek to hear His voice in the scriptures. We must learn to grab the moments to be in fellowship with Him whenever the opportunity affords itself, whether in the morning, afternoon, or evening. We must seek to hear His voice through the toughness or tenderness of our husband. We must seek to hear His voice through our husbands' love, and especially through his caring and wise counsel. We must remember that God is love. If He loved you enough to bless you with the gift of children, then He will see you though these rough times.

Yes, there will be tough times, but there are also the good times. There were precious moments when the babies learned to roll over, crawl, sit up, walk, feed themselves, or speak our names. There were seasons of chubby cheeks, the sweet baby smell, and the odiferous odors from filled diapers, the naps, the story times, or the getting together with other moms of little ones. There were the bad times too. The times when I felt like raising my voice or screaming out of frustration and I did. The times when I said unkind words or held an arm too tight out of anger. I'm so thankful that God forgives.

My advice on babies and toddlers is simply to love them. Diligently work at establishing a foundation of love, trust, security and respect in your relationship. Enjoy the various stages of growth with them while you can, for it sure doesn't last forever. Though when you're in the middle of them it seems like forever. Have fun!!!

Make it your goal to speak softly, touch gently, teach lovingly, and train with their future in mind. This is a wonderful period in their lives, when planting seeds of various kinds will grow for a lifetime. What do I mean by seeds you might ask? These are seeds from the Word of God of His redemptive plan, His love, His kindness, and His gentleness. Other seeds to cultivate are seeds of thought about life from your viewpoint and from every discipline known to man. This precious time can never be replaced.

The toddler years are great years for establishing patterns of self-discipline. This will begin as you organize your home. One of the first steps is setting up an orderly home is husband and wife deciding how things will operate. They must work toward everything having a place and everything being in its' place. (That works great for the first and second child, but by the time the third, fourth and fifth are coming along, sometimes it's hard to keep up with all the family dynamics going on.) Don't give up though. Things don't have to be perfect. Don't kill yourself trying to have the Better Homes and Garden look. There does need to be some semblance of order by which the family can operate and find the things necessary to function on a daily basis, but expecting perfection will invite frustration.

Establish a Biblical pattern for discipline. Dad and Mom should be reading and studying up on child discipline long before it is time to apply. This will help you as parents both work through some issues before appearing on opposite ends of the spectrum during a training moment or before you and the children are in the midst of a discipline crisis.

Establish good eating habits. Dad and Mom should make this a priority in their own lives first, since they will obviously be modeling this before the children. These earthly bodies are His Holy Temple so it is important what we put in them. Good nutrition is vitally important to health. . Especially when it comes to being able to process information in the brain. Good health will affect every facet of life.

Not only establish good eating habits but also establish good taste in music, radio, television and videos. There is not much redeemable on today's television but you can be selective with educational programming available. Here are some questions you might ask yourself? Does it glorify God? Does it teach anything about the Lord Jesus Christ? Does it lead to a deeper Christian walk? Does it teach subject matter that is beneficial to my growth as a person? Does it teach good character traits? Avoid the use of television as a babysitter, you must monitor everything! Remember, they model what the see and hear.

As the mother of a toddler, Mom will need lots of little breaks! It might be a trip to the grocery store, <u>ALONE,</u> or time to herself on a Saturday to shop, or an overnight retreat, or maybe time to visit with a friend. Moms need to find another mom going though the same thing for encouragement and validation that she's not alone. It is nice to have fellow travelers along the journey of life. This is where a home school support group can also be helpful or a church program like Mothers of Preschoolers (MOPS). Of course, we know Mom is not alone, the Spirit of God lives in her if she has Jesus as Lord and Savior.

Mom needs to take care for Mom. She needs to keep fit spiritually by spending time alone with God. She needs to stay focused on her husband by meeting his needs for respect, admiration, physical and sexual needs. She needs to eat healthy by making right food choices, eating proper portions, drinking plenty of water, and getting exercise. She can do this early before the children rise. She needs to take time with her general appearance with modest attractive clothing. She needs to nurture and care for the needs of her children. She also needs to get adequate rest.

> *"With toddlers, it is helpful to remember the Girl Scout motto: Be prepared! But it is probably most helpful to be flexible, patient, loving and kind! Most importantly, love them..."*

One mother found the following to be helpful- especially with several toddlers and younger school age children:

- Remember interruptions happen, they're a part of life.
    - Scale down and concentrate on the basics.
    - Reading opens a door to information. They can learn on their own.
    - We had toddlers be a part of our school, they are learning too.
    - Include them in "opening exercises."
- I tried to have a special individual time with toddlers after the "opening exercises" but before helping the older ones.
    - We made good use of meal times; I read special stories or gave information.
- We did "edible" Math.
    - Have special toys available only during school time.
- Also, it is extremely helpful to be prepared. Purchase the basic equipment and keep handy and available: Play Doh, Color Markers. Crayons, Large pencils, Pencil holders, Construction Paper, Glue, Stapler, Staples, Safe scissors. The month of July is a great month when school supplies are on sale in most stores. Buy early!

With toddlers, it is helpful to remember the Girl Scout motto: Be Prepared! But it is probably most helpful to be flexible, patient, loving and kind! Most importantly, love them.

Chapter 6

What Do I Teach?

"Teach me, O Lord, to follow your decrees;
Then I will keep them to the end.
Give me understanding,
And I will keep your law and obey it with all my heart.
Direct me in the path of your commands,
For there I find delight.
Turn my heart toward your statutes and not toward selfish gain.
Turn my eyes away from worthless things; preserve my life according to your word."
Psalm 119:33-37

"Teach us to number our days aright."
Psalm 90:12

"You must teach what is in accord with sound doctrine.
Teach the older men to be temperate, worthy of respect, self-controlled,
And sound in faith, in love and in endurance.
Likewise, teach the older women to be reverent in the way they live,
Not to be slanderers or addicted to much wine,
But to teach what is good.
Then they can train the younger women
To love their husbands and children,
To be self-controlled and pure,
To be busy at home, to be kind,
And to be subject to their husbands,
So that no one will malign the word of God."
Titus 2:1-5

There was a textbook giveaway at the warehouse for the local public school district. It was open to the public and as new home schoolers, we wanted to take advantage of all that we could. The children and I collected well over 200 books. After getting them home and unloading them, we began looking through the contents. There were some good older ones with teachings about language arts, grammar, geography, basic history or science. And then there were some that were full of fantasy, fiction and theories based mostly in Greek mythology.

I asked myself, *Is fantasy, fiction, or theories something we wanted to teach our children*? One day as I sat on the floor playing with the children, I began to contemplate our choices in education. First of all, I was overwhelmed by the thought of all that was out there to teach. Second, I felt a huge responsibility as a mother in the home because I would be the one there all day entrusted with the job of teaching. Third, I was frightened at the lack of accountability since no one else was behind our four walls to see exactly what we were doing. Fourth, I didn't know how we could truly measure whether or not the children were really learning what they were supposed to be learning.

As I continued in deeper reflection, I wondered to myself, *What about these Bible lessons I was teaching our children? Were they true? How did I really know if this was truth or fantasy? I had heard many of these stories all of my life. What if I were a Satanist or an atheist or an agnostic? Would I have a right to teach them those beliefs? Would we be brainwashing them if we only taught them our religion, from our denominational viewpoint? What about all the other ones out there? How did we know what was right to teach?*

Next, I began mentally listing my options about what to teach more than just academics. Children in the neighborhood were allowed to play with toy guns. *Should I allow mine to play with them? I could allow them to play with guns and learn to pretend shoot their friends or birds or holes in things. I could teach them to lie and never be able to trust them. I could teach them to steal and never be able to leave anything unlocked. I could teach them to fight to protect themselves or would they just become bullies? I could (not that I would) teach them to curse and use foul language but what purpose would it serve? I could (not that I would) teach them to commit indecent acts of sexual immorality, but what purpose would it serve and who would want diseases or who would want to marry them after that? I could teach them fantasy or fictitious stories or tell them about monsters that didn't exist, but I had already learned all too well about the fear that this created in my own life. Then I thought about simply teaching the facts. What if we just taught those things that were based on reality? What if we taught those things that could be proven, those things that were really true.*

I decided to take a mental walk along the lives of my parents, my siblings, Michaels' parents and his siblings, Michaels' life and my own. I thought about society, the problems that plagued society like abortion, alcoholism, drugs, sexual immorality, broken families, to name a few. I thought about the stories I read in the papers or saw on the news. I thought about our options to teach our children those things that would allow them to avoid the pitfalls of the previous generation. I thought about the options to teach our children those laws that would produce law-abiding, God-honoring citizens in our society. I thought about the children we would be proud to be the parents of. After reflecting and discussing all of this, Michael and I arrived at the conclusion of what we would teach…truth!

The decision was finalized one day when I heard a sweet, little voice of one of the children say "What's that?" I looked over to see a scorpion walking across the garage floor. "That!" I emphasized, "is a scorpion and it can sting. It will hurt very much!" After I said that so emphatically I realized that I didn't want to frighten them away from their interest of the beastly creature and I certainly didn't want to teach them fear. *Get a jar*! Something inside of me said. *What, are you crazy*? Something in me countered back. *Those little things sting*! I continued in thought. *Your children are watching! Do you want to teach them fear?* I stopped in my thought. "Humph… I can't believe I'm doing this…" I muttered out loud as I went to look for a jar.

It was time for me to put aside my squeamish anxiety and somehow muster up the courage to capture this critter for the sake of my children. I fought the fear inside of me as I quickly slammed the jar down over the scorpion. *I did it! I did it!* I thought with childish glee as my confidence was building. Next, with a careful, shaky hand, I slid a piece of paper slowly under the jar to form a seal. The paper became the lid as I flipped it over and watched the scorpion slide to the bottom of the jar. Now I screwed on the metal lid and poked a few air holes in it before taking it over to the children to view. For the rest of the afternoon, we observed the scorpion as it moved around the jar, flipping its tail up at times. The children wanted to know about it, so the next time we went to the library, we found books on insects, bugs and creepy critters.

There were other times when I found that "our" (Michael and my) behavior would be mirrored in our children. This made us further determine that whatever we taught, it should set a standard for doing what was right and true.

We learned that in their interactions with the neighborhood children they learned things quite quickly without "our" ever teaching them. We decided it was a good idea to teach them how to choose their friends.

In answering the question, "What do I Teach?" we determined that we would first begin with teaching how to love. In some ways this came naturally, in others it was a daily part of training in righteousness. There are many definitions of "love" in the world, but the true definition is: "God is love." This initial foundation of truth on love is found in I Corinthians 13:4-8, "Love is patient, love is kind. It does not envy, does not boast, is not proud. It is not rude, is not self-seeking, it is not easily angered, it keeps no records of wrong. Love does not delight in evil but rejoices with the truth. It always protects, always trusts, always hopes, and always perseveres. Love never fails."

Another passage, I Peter 4:8, describes love like this; "Love cover a multitude of sins." These verses are our model, yet we realize that only God can love like this. God in us has the power to love through us. In every situation in the home, the application of these passages is paramount to laying a good foundation. Love cannot be based on a child's looks, their behavior, their accomplishments or anything else. "God is love."

Next, we must teach good character. This training in character occurs in everyday life experiences, using good books (especially the Bible), videos or movies with moral lessons, or specific character training books. Character that should be purposely taught is:

Compassion	Enthusiasm	Obedience
Contentment	Faithfulness	Patience
Courage	Generosity	Purity
Decisiveness	Gentleness-Kindness	Responsibility
Dependability	Honesty	Reverence
Determination	Humility	Self-control
Diligence	Initiative	Tenderheartedness
Discernment	Integrity	Thankfulness
Discretion	Joyfulness	
Empathy	Loyalty	

It is also important to teach basic phonics. There are a number of phonics programs available and we tried several through the years. The one we found most thorough and effective was Writing Road To Reading by Romalda Spalding in conjunction with Teaching Reading At Home by Wanda Sanseri. With these programs, we introduced our children to the 70 basic phonograms (sounds that the letters make) and 1500 of the most commonly used words in the English language over a span of four to six years. Many programs limit children to grade appropriate basal readers or word families at a yearly progression. By using the <u>Writing Road To Reading,</u> once each phonogram is mastered, it provides a tool in the hands of the student to be able to decode individual words. In time, this frees the student up to read any level material including college levels. Following this program the students can go on to Latin vocabulary and Greek roots. During these foundational years, the children can be exposed to good reading material, with the Bible being foundational to all reading. Also, include dictionary work to study word meanings.

It is equally important for math to have a good foundation. Math should begin with the concrete (things you can see and touch) and move to abstract (numerical equations). For example, almost anything can be counted like apples, oranges, lampposts, street signs, rice, beans, pennies, etc. There are also some excellent math manipulatives on the market like Miquon math (there are many others) and of course there are computer programs that help a student visualize difficult concepts.

Once basic reading and math have been accomplished, the student can progress through other academic disciplines with ease (depending on their interests). They will not be restricted or limited by their inability to decode words, not understand them or not be able to visual math concepts in their brain.

There is no substitute for rigorous academic training. Repetition is the key to learning some material. For the home schooler, there is a constant tug of war between the discipline versus the undisciplined approach. A field trip out of the house will always sound better than sitting down to do schoolwork. Balance is the key. Praying, planning and scheduling will be keys to finding balance. Watch out for the time wasters! The media/technology explosion via the introduction of Internet, computers, videos, Nintendo, Arcade games, handheld games, and the increase in sports' activity outside of the home, have all contributed to the downfall in the discipline of good study habits.

"Curriculum purchased is not necessarily curriculum used," said one mother, so do not expect to find a perfect curriculum to teach. As another mother said, "Anything works if the teacher works."

Quite early in our home schooling adventure, we learned that we could not possibly teach our children everything that they needed to know. God created them. He knew how He had designed them and for what purpose. As we observed each of our children, the Lord gave us wisdom on what was important to teach them (especially the discerning wife who spends a great deal of time with the children). But the Lord taught me the importance of going to my husband as the authority in our home before the implementation of any teaching or field trip activity.

It is important for fathers to be involved in teaching little boys good character, how to love, how to play, how to lose, how to succeed, how to work, how to get up when they fail, and how to grow up to become men. It is important that they be exposed to other boys and men of good character in their neighborhood, church, community and world.

It is important for mothers to be involved in teaching little girls good character, how to love, how to be dainty, how to play, how to lose, how to succeed, how to work, how to get up when they fail, how to grow up to become women. It is important that they be exposed to other girls and women of good character in the neighborhood, church, community and world.

It is also important to teach them about allegiance. First, teach allegiance to God, then family, church, community and country. It is important to teach the disciplined life: self-control in many areas, time with the Lord, anger and its' expression, finance, eating, material possessions, self-gratification, etc. It is important to teach how to love one another throughout one's lifespan upon this earth.

It is important to teach children the reality of God. Though they cannot see Him, He exists and is in complete control. It is important to teach the reality of Jesus. He is alive and at the right hand of the Father, He is making intercession for us. It is important to teach the reality of God with us. Jesus promised the Holy Spirit before He ascended back into heaven. The Spirit of the Living God is here. He is in us, with us and is a friend that sticks closer than a brother.

Chapter 7

How To Find Your Way Through the Curriculum Maze

"The goal of our instruction
Is love
From a pure heart
And a good conscience
And a sincere faith."
1 Timothy 1:5

"Ask and it will be given to you;
Seek and you will find;
Knock and the door will be opened to you.
For everyone who asks receives;
He who seeks finds;
And to him who knocks
The door will be opened."
Matthew 7:7,8

I n 1988, Michael got a job working in the Pentagon. There was time enough to get the family settled in a house and to make a few trips into Washington D. C. But after that one week, he went back to work and I was on my own to learn how to get around the area. His parents decided to come for a visit. Since Michael could not get away from work to pick them up, I needed to do it. He went over directions with me the night before on how to get there. The next morning, fear and panic set in as I thought about negotiating traffic, finding the airport, finding his parents, and having four little ones to control. Washington International Airport is both large and busy.

I did well until I reached Crystal City, which is located right near the airport. I followed all the airport signs, but after a series of turns, lost my way. I began to turn corners. I turned some corners enough times that they soon became recognizable and I knew not to go down them again. The children were trying to help. It was our eight-year-old son Michael who pointed out the fact that we had tried all the streets except one. We took it and arrived at the airport. What does this story have to do with home schooling you ask?

Home schooling can be just like a maze at times. You can read all the books on home education, know where you want to go, but at some point become confused. The children change. Your situation changes. You change. Your husband changes. Maybe you can't keep up with the curriculum. Maybe your child gets stuck on a concept. The methods may change, but remember the goal is to help our children be the type of people who love the Lord and seek Him. He never changes.

> ## *"Should I go with A Beka, Bob Jones, Christian Light, Alpha Omega, Hewitt, Konos, Ann Ward, Bill Gothard? Do I try Unit Studies or go with a more traditional approach?"*

Whether you're new to home schooling or you've done it for many years, home schooling can really be confusing with the varied choices in curriculum and educational philosophies. If you keep asking, seeking, and searching, God will give you wisdom. That's a promise. (James 1:5)

I'll never forget the feeling I had standing there in the doorway of the convention hall several years after my airport fiasco, thankful to have so many choices, yet in awe of the number of vendors selling their wares. There were booths for T-shirts, dresses, new books, used books, tapes, college representatives, computer programs, paper, and more books. There was a booth on Eating Right and another selling bread machines with samples available. I had attended several workshops already and my mind was in a spin. *So many opinions, so many different philosophies*, I thought. I felt a strong overwhelming feeling of confusion and oppression. *If I feel like this after thirteen years of home schooling, I can only imagine what other home schoolers must feel like. Should I go with A Beka, Bob Jones, Christian Light, Alpha Omega, Hewitt, Konos, Ann Ward, Bill Gothard? Do I try Unit Studies or go with a more traditional approach? What is best for our family, our children and our budget?*

One of the most important lessons we have learned is to let the Holy Spirit be our guide. Since God is the designer and creator of us all, it only made sense for us to go to Him to ask for help. In the early years, I wrote down each of the children's names in the back of my Bible. As the Lord would impress something about that child upon my mind and heart, I wrote it down. As I observed them in play or interactions with others, I jotted down their strengths and weaknesses, their likes and dislikes. I then found creative ways to address their needs. I would purchase certain books according to their interests or maybe a magazine subscription in that particular field of interest. I would sign them up for classes or hire a tutor if Michael or myself were unable to teach a particular subject.

We learned to set realistic goals and objectives for each individual child. We learned to allow our children to work at their own pace. We discovered that trying to force our children to learn invited anger, frustration and resistance into the learning experience.

Our family's educational philosophy helped us to focus our attention on what was important to us. This helped to eliminate unnecessary curriculum purchases. By understanding our own learning style, we were able to better help our children. By understanding our children's learning style, we were able to tap into a resource with unlimited potential. We allowed them to develop their strengths and work on their weaknesses. The beauty of home schooling is the advantage of tailor making curriculum to the individual needs of your child and the uniqueness of your family situation…

Your child should be one of the first steps in designing an individual program. An assessment is necessary to determine on which skill level the child is working. There have been many parents who give no consideration to their child, their situation, or their budget. They simply ordered the curriculum without forethought to these variables. Then they wonder why home schooling is not working for them. To help determine answers to the question "What's best for us?" listed below are a few ideas:

1. Pray together as a couple and as a family, ask God for guidance
2. Take one day at a time
3. Visit the library for books on Home Schooling
4. Visit your local Christian bookstore
5. Study home school catalogs, brochures
6. Talk with other home schoolers
7. Attend local support group meetings
8. Attend Curriculum /Book Fairs
9. Attend a State Convention

Questions to answer to help determine what's best for each of our children:

1. What is unique to our family situation? (i.e. Father's profession)

2. What are our goals, purpose & objectives? (i.e. Why are we doing this?)

3. What is our family's educational philosophy? Write it down as you brainstorm.

4. What learning styles do we as parents have? (The Way They Learn by Cynthia Tobias)

5. What is each child's learning style? (The Way They Learn by Cynthia Tobias)

6. What is our education budget? (i.e. How much can we afford?)

7. What are our curriculum choices according to our philosophy, learning styles, finances?

8. How should we assess our child? (Spiritually, academically, physically, emotionally) (Academic Testing/Portfolio/Medical)

Everyone would love to find that "perfect" curriculum. But there is not one to be found. There is no school public, private or home school that has one. Only God can show you the way for your family. By abiding in Christ, the Holy Spirit will guide you into all truth. There is absolutely no substitute for learning to daily trust in the Lord and in His provision for your home school except to daily walk with Him. God has a purpose and a plan for each individual placed in your family. No child is there by accident.

Nephew Shaun & the Cross Family visit Busch Gardens

Cross Family Educational Philosophy

I. We believe that both the Old and New Testaments are the inspired Word of God, revealing the three Persons of the Godhead: Father, Son and Holy Spirit. (Genesis 1:1; Acts 1:1-9; 7:1-56)

II. We believe in the incarnation and virgin birth of our Lord and Saviour Jesus Christ as true God and true man. (Matthew 1:1-25; Romans 1:3,4; 4:21-25)

III. We believe that man was created in the image of God, but is separated from God by sin. (Genesis 1:26,27; Romans 3:23-25)

IV. We believe that man is redeemed by grace through faith in Christ's vicarious atonement for sins, the shedding of His blood on the cross. (Romans 5:8,9)

V. We believe that the gift of eternal life is available to all men, that those who receive Christ by faith are regenerated by the Holy Spirit and thereby become children of God. (Romans 5:8-21)

VI. We believe in the bodily Resurrection of Christ, His imminent return, and the resurrection of His people. (Acts 1:1-11; I Thessalonians 4:13-18)

VII. We believe children are gifts from God. We believe children belong to God, not the state. God entrusts parents for the care and training of their children. (Genesis 33:5, 48:8-9, I Samuel 1:20, Psalm 24:1, Psalm 113:9, Psalm 127:3, Isaiah 8:18, Isaiah 29:23)

VIII. We believe God has given parents, not the state, the authority and responsibility to educate their children. (Genesis 18:19, Deuteronomy 11:18-20; 32:45,46; Psalm 34:11; 78:1-11, Proverbs 1:8; 2:1-5; 3:12; 4:1; 4:20-27; 22:6; Joel 1:3; I Thessalonians 2:11)

IX. We believe education is a duty which parents owe to God alone. This duty, and the manner of discharging it, is a matter of the heart and mind. It is enforceable only by the sword of the Spirit. Parents are under no obligation to submit to state regulation of duties owed exclusively to God. The apostles were commanded by Jesus to go and teach all nations. Yet, in Acts 5, when the apostles were forbidden to teach without the approval of the Sanhedrin, they replied, "We must obey God rather than men!" Thus, parents who teach their children at home according to their convictions are not breaking the law. They are obeying a higher law.

X. We believe God is the author of all truth. All wisdom and knowledge come from the Lord. His Word is the measure of all things. (Psalm 111:10; 36:9; 86:11; 119:151; Isaiah 55:8,9; Proverbs 1:7; John 14:6; 16:13; 17:17; Colossians 2:2,3; I Timothy 3:16; James 1:5; I John 5:20)

XI. We believe since all wisdom and knowledge are hidden in Christ, truth cannot be distinguished as religious and non-religious.

XII. We believe God's truth encompasses the totality of life and the created order. He created the universe and the physical laws which govern it. Thus, the study of mathematics and science begins with God, the Creator. God created men, nations, time, and history. Thus, the study of subjects such as history, law, and government is predicated upon the fact that God is intimately involved in the affairs of men and nations. God created man in His own image with similar creative and expressive abilities. Thus, we imitate God in pursuing fields such as art, communication, and the humanities. All knowledge should be centered on Christ Jesus, the one "in whom are hidden all the treasures of wisdom and knowledge."

XIII. We believe the goal of education should be to raise a faithful, wise and God-fearing servant of the Lord. The servant should be able to show himself approved and equipped to carry out the Cultural Mandate (Genesis 1:26-28) and the Great Commission (Matthew 28:18-20)

Chapter 8

A Home Educated Child

Leads A More Educated Parent

"A student is not above his teacher, nor a servant above his master.
It is enough for the student to be like his teacher, and the servant like his master."
Matthew 10:24

O ne early morning I received a phone call from a friend in my church. We were both members of Concerned Women For America (CWA), an organization started by Tim and Beverly LaHaye, dedicated to preserving Christian family values. Amanda had received word that CWA was calling a news conference in one of the Senate office buildings called the Russell Building in downtown Washington D.C. to express their support for Judge Clarence Thomas, a nominee for the Supreme Court. Sparks were beginning to fly concerning allegations made by a former employee. There were rumors of accusations launched against him by a woman named Anita Hill.

Amanda was a young mother with twin babies and I was a home schooling mother with four young children who wanted to take advantage of every opportunity to utilize teachable moments in the lives of my children. For me, it was a grand opportunity for us to see the real political process firsthand. She decided to leave her little ones at home. We both decided it would be worth the trip into downtown. We managed to find our way through the busy streets of Washington D.C. and find parking on a side street. We were amazed at the number of people already there protesting both for and against Judge Thomas. There were news reporters and cameramen cluttering the walkways and doorways. It was all we could do to stay out of the paths of the crowds as we waited for the building to be opened for the special news conference.

Having never seen anything like this before in my life, I was excited. This was my first time entering a government building on this grand of a scale, with security guards and scanning machines! I knew the children had no idea that they were actually taking part in a historical event that would someday be recorded in history books. We watched as radio reporters walked around thrusting mikes before various individuals in the crowds, and then suddenly without warning, one was thrust before me. "Why are you here?" the reporter asked. Thinking quickly I said, "We are home schoolers and we wanted to show our support of Judge Thomas." He then leaned down to ask one of the children a question. My heart throbbed as I realized that whatever came out of that little mouth would be broadcast "live" all over some radio station. I don't recall exactly what my child said, but I was relieved after they spoke. The interview went very well.

The Russell Building was opened up and we squeezed our way through with all the other people. The room was packed with people as tight as sardines are in a can. As one of the leaders of CWA made her way by us, I asked if it were possible for my children and I to stand in the back of the room and listen. "In the back?" she asked, "No," she said kindly, "I saw you and your family earlier and I was looking for you. I want you and the children to stand right up front!" She led the way through the crowd and there we were standing next to the podium, under the bright lights of the cameras. The first speaker began to voice her support of Judge Thomas. How thrilling that was for me, an adult and for the children to see this aspect of our nation's political process "the exercise of our 1st Amendment rights."

After the news conference, we were ushered into the hallway to await Judge Thomas' arrival. While we waited someone ran through the halls passing out white T-shirts with red lettering stating, "Taking a stand for righteousness and for Thomas." We quickly pulled the t-shirts over our heads. Then without warning a throng of reporters, cameramen, and whomever else was in the crowd burst through like a whirlwind. It was all I could do to hold onto my children so that the crowd would not crush them. While we were plastered against the wall, I saw a flash of Judge Thomas as his head whizzed by through the madness. This was an experience I as an adult, will never forget. Of course, as we headed home, we turned on the radio and listened to the beginning of Miss Hill's testimony. We felt sickened and disheartened. What an education we received that day and in the days to follow…

As a home educator, I found myself being "stretched" out of my comfort zone. Michael and I had gone to public schools where everything had been arranged for us. We were given books and told what to study and when to take the test. Now, in order to best serve our children, we were forced to ask questions, schedule field trips, read road maps, navigate through highways and side streets, drive through large cities and small towns, do research on topics, study and prepare for lessons, and work to understand subjects and administer tests. When problems arose, Michael and I had to deal with them as a couple and seek the best solution as a family. We found ourselves going places and doing things we had never imagined. Our family went on field trips to places that we only read about as children.

> ***Home schooling forced us to become better teachers... Home schooling forced us to be exposed to different philosophies of education, different methods of teaching, different learning styles of students. Home schooling forced us to learn.***

When we studied various subjects, we made them come alive by visiting the sites. When we studied the past, we visited a local farm and milked a cow, toured a garden of herbs and took a hayride. When we studied science, we toured a nature center or maybe a pumpkin patch. When we studied the Civil War we visited several locations of the Manassas battlefield. We traveled with others home schooling families to Appomattox where Lee surrendered to Grant. We visited Gettysburg where Lincoln gave his famous speech "The Gettysburg Address" and we grimaced at the number of tombstones that represented the enormous loss of life which bought our freedom. We toured The Ford Theater where Lincoln was shot. We scheduled group field trips to the FBI building, the National Aquarium, Mount Vernon-George Washington's home, Williamsburg. We drove to Fort McHenry and viewed the film where Francis Scott Key penned the words to "The Star Spangled Banner" while being held captive in a boat sitting in the harbor. We stood where many famous gatherings have been held at the top of the steps of the Lincoln Memorial. We somberly strolled past the Tomb of the Unknown Soldier in Arlington Cemetery. We ran around with glee at an Easter egg hunt on the front lawn of the White House. We visited the Art Factory and saw great works of art from the past and in the making. On one field trip, we sat in a police cruiser amazed at all the gadgets, learned about drugs legally, and went behind bars temporarily at the police station. On another trip, we walked into the vault of the bank and didn't get locked in or arrested. We parents received quite an education!

As home educators, we became involved in community service projects. For one, we visited the nursing homes. We especially loved Christmas time to bring little gifts, cheer, songs and music. Lots of groups did that and we learned that residents were very lonely during the year, so we took it one step further. We would take them to doctor or dental appointments in our car. While we waited for one of the residents, the children and I read books in the car or they did their schoolwork. I was able to converse with the elderly as I drove and glean wisdom. Few, if any, talked about the jobs they once held. Most talked about their families. Some expressed much love and tenderness in remembering their loved ones and some such bitterness. Most encouraged me to love my children. Most told me that when you are old you will need, them. Some when asked for wisdom had none or couldn't remember. Some encouraged me to "never give up!" We parents received quite an education!

A Visit to Williamsburg

A Visit to Bible Land USA in Virginia

Home educating forced us to keep learning. There was a need to test my children for our own assessment and as a requirement for the state. Since testers were required to have college degrees, this encouraged me to pursue and complete one. I also hoped to use it for future income. The Lord, my husband and children opened the doors for me to pursue a degree. I was able to accomplish this with the help of family and friends. I learned quickly that I could not do it all, home school and go to school. So I learned to prioritize. I learned to set limits, drop unnecessary activities and use my time wisely. The Lord enabled me to graduate with a Bachelor's degree in Church Ministries with a minor in Educational ministries from Liberty University in May 1991 as a more educated parent "on paper." But it was the "real life" education of meeting people from different walks of life, sharing experiences, learning together, traveling, seeing, and doing that I received from home schooling that taught me many invaluable lessons.

Home educating forced us to keep abreast of our child's progress. Daily lessons revealed their weaknesses and their strengths. Home educating forced us to think, plan, execute and work together as a family. Home educating forced to socialize with others and to network for various reasons. Home educating forced us to know the laws, to become involved in the political process. Home educating forced us to get out and vote to make our selection of candidates who upheld our values. Home educating forced us to think and thus make wiser decisions. Home schooling forced us to be thrifty and frugal with the use of our dollars for curriculum. Home educating forced us to discern that which was good and beneficial from that which was a time waster or evil. Home educating forced us to keep healthy to meet the needs of our growing family. Home schooling forced us to learn better parenting skills. Home schooling forced us to become better teachers and communicators. Home schooling forced us to check out the many educational choices ad options that were available. Home schooling forced us to learn educational jargon, terminology and practices. Home schooling forced us to be exposed to different philosophies of education, different methods of teaching, different learning styles of students. Home schooling forced us to learn. We parents received quite an education! For us, home schooling led to more educated parents.

Liberty University in May 1991

Chapter 9

How Do You Spell Relief?

D-e-s-e-r-t-e-d I-s-l-a-n-d

"Come to me, all you who are weary and burdened, and I will give you rest.
Take my yoke upon you and learn from me, for I am gentle and humble in heart,
And you will find rest for your souls.
For my yoke is easy and my burden is light."
Matthew 11:28

He who dwells in the shelter of the Most High
Will rest in the shadow of the Almighty.
I will say of the Lord,
"He is my refuge and my fortress, my God,
In whom I trust."
Psalm 91:1,2

ne morning after Michael left for work, I found a card on the dining room table. The front of the card made me want to jump right into the middle of the beach scene. There was the beautiful blue water, the sandy beach and a nice palm tree in the background. On the inside of the card were these words: "I'd love to get lost on an island with you, just the two of us." I sighed… *Wouldn't that be nice,"* I thought. I knew his work at the Pentagon was getting tougher and the stress was taking its' toll on my husband. I sat the card back down on the table.

When the children came down to breakfast, Janet inquired about the card. "Oh, is this a card from Daddy?" she asked. "Yes," I countered, "Poor thing! He's having a hard time at work and wants to get away to a deserted island." I smiled and added a little chuckle. She didn't answer. It was obvious by the look on her face that her brain was engaged in some heavy-duty thinking. "I have an idea," she said and off she disappeared into the basement. The other children had come into the room while Janet and I talked, they too began to get some ideas of their own. I watched as each of them raced in different directions of the house. For a moment, I thought I had lost total control, and I had.

The children were moving about the house and returning to the kitchen with various objects. "What are you doing?" I asked, as one child brought in an old piece of blue carpet. "This can be the water," he said. Another brought the Fichus tree from the living room, "This is the palm tree!" Mark had gone out to the back of the house to gather wood to make a pretend tripod on the carpet as if over a fire. Right in the middle of the chaos, the phone rang. It was Linda, another home schooling mom from my support group.

I couldn't help but laugh as I told her what the children were doing; they had taken Daddy's request literally! When she heard what my creative children were doing, she thought it was a wonderful idea, and began to throw in a few of her own. "I have a bottle of pineapple drink," she said. Next, she suggested that I bring my children over to her house later on in the afternoon so that Michael and I could enjoy a quiet evening on our deserted island. I hung up the phone, wondering if I had lost my mind. We hadn't even started on our academics!

By that evening, the children were having a great time at Linda's. On the way back home, I picked up a large fresh fish and a few items to complete our tropical theme. Before he arrived, I made a banner for him to read as he entered the door. Lastly, I completed the picture by dressing up for the part. He came home to an island girl. What a spectacular end to a tough day for him and a rearranged day for me! The next afternoon, when we went to pick the children up, we received another unexpected blessing. While our husbands talked to one another, Linda and I talked in the kitchen and the children played. No one paid close enough attention to the snow quietly falling outside. Finding ourselves snowed in, we spent the night playing games, talking and sharing lives. We still hold these memories dear to our heart…

> However you spell relief is fine!
> Just make sure you get some…

Throughout my home schooling years, relief usually came when Daddy got home. Michael was always gracious and understanding of the difficulty I faced as a mother in the home with the constant care of children all day long. Relief came in many, many forms. There were times when he sent me straight to my room, and I crashed into the bed. There were times when he allowed me to finish a sewing project or a project around the house. Once he even allowed me to add two layers of brick to an existing brick wall. There were times when he would tell me to take a class on something I liked to do, like tole painting or a First Aid course. There were times when he sent me off on a ladies retreat or to home schooling seminars. There were times when he allowed me to do one-on-one Bible studies with another mother at night while he was home to watch our children. There were times when he gave me the money to simply go shopping or do something for myself.

You can't home school for very long without realizing that Mom needs an occasional break.

One unexpected blessing of relief came when a support group we started sent us off to a little retreat. They arranged to watch and care for the children during that time.

In later years of home schooling, I arranged weekend retreats for the home schooling mothers in our support group. Sometimes I arranged weekend getaways for just Michael and I. Sometimes I arranged for daylong trips to a mall with several other mothers. There were times when we hosted "couple's dinners" in our home or a video series on marriage. However you spell relief is fine! Just make sure you get some...

The Mothers of Knollwood Home School Support Group

Chapter 10

Be Available for Ministry

"A new command give you: Love one another.
As I have loved you, so you must love one another.
By this all men will know that you are my
Disciples."
John 13:35

I stood by my window looking out. Emotion welled inside me as I glanced back toward the front page of the Washington Post. A tear rolled down my cheek as I thought about another young black man slain and the picture of his body lying just below the headlines, again. *What a waste of human life*! I thought. *Such potential. This person was some mothers' child. This person was somebody's brother, or uncle, or father. O God, what can I do*?

I thought about the times our family had stood on the ellipse in front of the White House and marched down Pennsylvania Avenue to the Supreme Court. We carried our signs and made our statement. But as we rode back home on the Metro, I wondered if we had really made any difference. *What about foster care?* I thought, No*! There is no way I could give them back - too unstable of a lifestyle for our family, I* answered myself. *Maybe adoption? No, our children were still young and we had four already.*

Several months later, God answered that prayer. It was the first day of pool season and the first time I was free—free from having to stand in the water with Jennifer and Janet. They were six now and could play in the three feet and under side of the pool by themselves. I was actually elated that I no longer had a diaper bag, stroller, or baby to worry about. So, I sat the beach bag down and positioned myself comfortably. I no sooner lay my head back onto the chaise lounger than Sue walked up.

"Hi!" Sue said. "Hi!" I answered. Staring up into her protruding abdomen, I could see that she was obviously pregnant. We met the summer before at the very same pool. Her husband was in the Marines and led an Officer's Christian Fellowship Bible Study. We chatted for a few minutes and before she left, she asked if I knew any Black families in our church that might want to adopt. She told me of a couple in her church needing a home for a child in foster care.

My heart melted inside. While the children played, I kept thinking about this child that needed a home. God had richly blessed us, and even if we were in a rental home, it was our home-surely we could share out of that abundance. I decided to call the agency when we got back home. Pat, of Bethany Christian Services was very gracious, but she had no idea which child I was talking about. Before I knew it, she was asking me all kinds of questions about our family. "Mrs. Cross," she said after we had conversed for several minutes, "I don't know which child it is you're referring to, but we have lots of babies that need homes." One of the last questions she asked was, "How many children do you have?" When I said "four," it abruptly ended the conversation. "Thank you for calling," she said. *O.K. Lord*, I thought, Y*ou closed that door*.

When Michael returned home, I told him of my conversation and we pretty much decided that was the end of it. Three weeks later, Pat called, "If you're still willing, I am" she said. We started the process and one month later on September 27, 1989 we brought our son Matthew Allan home. Two years after that, by faith, I placed an empty box on a closet shelf. On the outside of the box, I wrote the name: Micah Andrew. I spent the next year collecting baby clothes in it. We waited and waited. When we thought we had run out of time for adopting again, we decided to remove our names from the waiting list on December 1st, 1992. On November 30th, 1992, we received a call to pick up our son, Micah Andrew.

Ministry was learning to hear the voice of God on a daily basis as we read His Word and applied the principles and truths we learned, right where we lived.

There were other times opportunities too. Like the time we lived in Las Vegas when my friend Jan and I were finishing up our Bible study together. Suddenly my front door burst open. The previously happy atmosphere with children quietly playing and two mothers talking was shattered with screams of "Help me! My baby's turning blue!" Kim was frantic, as she shoved Adam into my arms. Life seemed to come to a stand still except for the little purpled lipped baby and me. I held him slightly upside down and did a finger sweep of his mouth hoping to find an item if he were choking. But I found nothing. "Do CPR!" Kim screamed at me! But all the while God's spirit in me gave me the presence of mind to assess the situation. *A-airway, B-breathing, C-circulation*, was going through my mind. "Children pray," I stated firmly but calmly, while Kim continued to go to pieces on me. Without even asking, Jan had run next door to find Kim's daughter Ashley.

I proceeded to lay the baby Adam down on the cold, hard counter top and to call 911. By the time the ambulance attendants arrive, little Adam was no longer purple and blue. He appeared to be back to normal. Later, after a visit to the emergency room, Kim learned that Adam had a double ear-infection. His temperature had risen so fast that he experienced a febrile seizure. Lying there on that cold counter was the best thing for him.

Through the years, our family ministered to Karen, a young single woman who needed a place to live for a few months. We ministered to Brenda, whose husband was an unbeliever and needed a listening ear. We ministered to Melissa, a young mother who needed someone to watch her little girls for an afternoon. We ministered to Kim who needed to know how to get started home schooling. We ministered to Betty who needed encouragement. We ministered to Joe and Gina, to Danny and Judy, to Keith and Waynette, to elderly neighbors Wally and Sylvia. We ministered to Jackie, our sister, a single parent and her son Shaun. We ministered to the home school support group, to the Sunday school class. We ministered to whomever God led our way.

Home schooling allowed us many, many, many opportunities for ministry. We learned that ministry was not just at church. Ministry was not a full time position on staff somewhere. We were in full time ministry, operating right out of our home. We ministered to lost and saved neighbors, fellow home schoolers, and believers from church, people we met on the street in everyday life, our family and friends. Ministry was learning to hear the voice of God on a daily basis as we read His Word and applied the principles and truths we learned—right where we lived.

As time passed, we saw God expand our ministry opportunities through our individual gifts, talents and abilities. Notice the word "TIME." That tiny little four-letter word is critical and important. Ministry takes time. Families take time also. That is why, listening to the One who knows no beginning or end of time; the Alpha and Omega is so important. It is in taking one day at a time and leaving the results to Him that is paramount.

Chapter 11

Learning From Your Children

"Even a child is known by his actions by whether his conduct is pure and right."
Proverbs 20:11

W e pulled into the driveway of Mr. Lenny Seidel, an extraordinarily gifted and talented piano player. It was time for Michael's lesson. Just as I slid the gearshift indicator into park, twelve-year-old Michael suddenly yelled, "Mommy! There's a snake!" "Where?" I gasped. "Over there in the grass," he said as he raced out of the car. He ran over to the spot where he saw the snake, but no snake could be found. Michael abandoned the snake finding mission and disappeared into Lenny's home.

I watched as the door closed behind him and settled back in my seat after that hair-raising experience. Eleven-year-old Mark, nine-year-old twins Jennifer and Janet, and three-year-old Matthew loved this time because I used it to tell them made-up stories while we waited for Michael's piano lesson to be over. I was about to begin a story when the silence was broken once again with "There he is!" Mark yelled as he leaped from the car and returned to the exact location Michael had previously seen the so-called snake. I watched Mark as he slowly and methodically took each step attempting to make a surprise capture. *He did see a snake*! I thought. Now I saw the snake. It was slithering along into the chunks of brown mulch when Mark lunged forward and grabbed it. Slowly I let his name roll off my lips. "Mmmammarrkkk, dooo yoouuu knowww what kind of snake that is? My heart was racing. I leaned further out of the car window but he didn't hear me. He was too engrossed in admiring his prize. "This is number five," he stated proudly.

Before I knew it, he had made his way across several feet of lawn to thrust the snake right in front of me. "Gggget -t-tttt that snake away from me!" I stammered. He backed up. "Mommy, did you know this is a female snake?" Mark asked. "As a matter-of-fact I didn't know that," I answered rather sarcastically, "I've never taken the time to get that close."

"Just how do you know?" I asked. "Well," he said with such authority, "do you see this slit?" I peered over cautiously. "Yes." "Well, that's where the eggs come from," he said. Now I was curious and nervous all at the same time. "Do you know what kind of snake that is?" I asked. "You know it could be poisonous." "Oh, it's not poisonous," he quickly spoke up, "I can tell by the shape of its' head."

Without any fear, he began to open the snakes' mouth as it coiled around his little finger. I watched as the snake kept sticking its' long, black tongue out at me. "Mommy?" Mark asked as he awakened me from my intense focus on that tongue, "Did you know a snake could open its' mouth like this?" He took his hand and stretched the mouth of the snake far apart…

I was learning from my child. Not only did he not fear this reptile, but also he had learned information from his self-initiated exposure to snakes while visiting museums and nature centers. He also read books and encyclopedias. Daily, it was becoming more apparent to me that I was a student of my child.

The Unexpected Burn

One day, my husband, received orders to transfer to Wright Patterson Air Force Base in Dayton Ohio. A few days before the packers were to come, I decided to take a break from cooking by purchasing those inexpensive sodium filled delicious potpies. We loved those little pies, especially the ones with a bottom and top crust. I baked them and sat the golden brown pies one by one on top of the stove to cool.

After a few minutes, I began to transport each pie onto a plate destined for the table and our hungry mouths. But in the flash of a moment, one of the pies started to slip and slide, then it suddenly flipped over into the air. Without thinking, I reached to catch it. The crispy brown crust rapidly broke into a thousand pieces quickly oozing the boiling hot contents all over my right hand. I cried out in pain and ran for the sink. I turned on the cold water and let it run. I hoped the coolness of the water would sooth the burn but the pain was so excruciating that I began to weep loudly.

The children each responded to this sudden confusion in their own way. Nine-year-old Jennifer immediately ran to my side and wrapped her merciful arms around me. She held on to me for dear life and it was comforting. "Oh Mommy!" she uttered painstakingly and tried to console me. My tenderhearted, barefooted, clingy three-year-old Matthew made an attempt to run to me in the midst of this chaos, but he neglected to notice the scalding contents of the chicken potpie splattered on the floor. Stepping directly in it, he began running, hopping on one foot and yelling all around the room. "Ouch! Ouch!" Matthew yelled.. At this point, my focus was off of my hand and onto Matthew, while the tears continued to roll down my cheek. "Somebody—wash—off— his— foot!" I managed to call out between sniffles and my own sobs due to the pain in my hand.

Nine-year-old Janet helped her brother Matthew and then took a broom and began to clean up the mess. Mark, our eleven-year-old ran straight to the freezer, grabbed a bowl of ice (my neighbor had come over that very same afternoon and given me four ice trays since she too was moving.) The ice trays were filled with partially frozen water. He threw the ice in a bowl, filled it with water and shoved my hand into it. He then went back to watching a program on the television. Twelve-year-old Michael ran to the first aid kit. He pulled out the American Red Cross booklet and found a chart that explained what to do about burns. "Mommy," he said, "You need to…" and he read off the listed information.

Later, reflecting back over that event, I marveled at the way each child responded. I learned that each of my children is wired differently. I learned that it is possible for them to be trained to respond in a certain way during certain situations, but it was just plain funny to think about what I had learned from the way they responded to my unexpected burn.

As the children grew, it was both beautiful and wonderful to see all of us learning, growing and sharing our knowledge with one another. Michael Christopher grew in his knowledge of music. He took piano lessons from Dr. Clevenger, the chairman of the Music Department of Cedarville College. His hobby became the computer. He soon became our personal computer consultant. He was dedicated and determined. At age sixteen, he spent an entire day assembling and installing our new garage door opener. Mark Anthony grew to be the warrior/protector. He was the one we called on when we discovered a mole, raccoon, snake, sheep and goats that were out of the pen or anything else we couldn't handle. He was quick and witty. He amazed us with his artistic ability to design gadgets from the most common of household objects. He was also the shepherd boy. He could be so tender as he helped to birth a newborn lamb or tough as he dealt with our ram Lambert who often charged at him. Jennifer exposed us to great works of literature. She could never seem to put a book down. After hearing missionary stories and reading a book entitled The First Woman

<u>Doctor</u> by Elizabeth Blackwell, Jennifer at age five decided to become a doctor. She always carried herself as a dainty lady well beyond her years of age. Janet, the artist, taught herself to draw and paint. She even taught herself to cook and sew. Even though many of her early sewing creations no one could wear, she eventually developed masterpieces. She could cut the fabric and stitch something together in an evening. As both she and Jennifer grew older, they became like second mothers to our younger sons. At times, this was both a blessing and a curse. When the younger boys listened and obeyed, the girls' help was a blessing. But when Matthew and Micah didn't show respect for their authority and they argued back, the friction caused between the siblings felt like a curse. Matthew was the one who constantly desired to be at his mother's side. He was sensitive, discerning, and impulsive. Micah was the little professor in constant motion. The throttle speed on him was locked in the "Fast" position. He was always begging to do an experiment. We usually found them in the freezer.

My husband Michael and I could not know everything in this vast world of growing knowledge. We didn't have to. God had given these children each a brain and as they used this marvelous gift, we saw the value in our differences and the value in how much they were teaching us. Not only did we gain from their academic pursuits but more importantly, we gained from them spiritually. We discovered that our children painted a symbolic portrait of our relationship with God. They taught us lessons that no book could even teach. How convicting and inspiring!

Our Visit To The White House

Chapter 12

What About Socialization?

He said to them: "It is not for you to know the times or dates the Father has set by His own authority.
But you will receive power when the Holy Spirit comes on you;
And you will be my witnesses in Jerusalem, and in all Judea and Samaria, and to the ends of the earth."
Acts 1:7,8
"I have written you in my letter not to associate with sexually immoral people—not at all meaning the people
of this world who are immoral, or the greedy and swindlers, or idolaters. In that case you would have to leave
this world. But now I am writing you that you must not associate with anyone who calls himself a brother but
is sexually immoral or greedy, an idolater or a slanderer, a drunkard or a swindler. With such a man do not
even eat."
I Corinthians. 5:9-13

The Early Years

ell me Mrs. Cross, what about socialization?" Mrs. Raymore asked as we sat in a room full of relatives and friends of my husband parents. I had never met nor did I know many of these relatives. Michael and I had flown from Las Vegas to Florida with our four children ages six and under for a visit. Michaels' mother arranged to entertain over twenty-five guests in honor of her son and his family's visit. Mrs. Raymore continued, "Your children have never been to school?" she asked, "How will they be able to relate to people?" I paused and looked around the room to see where the children were. I quickly spotted each child. "Where are my children now?" I asked her. She then stopped to look for them. She looked at them and then at me. She was amazed. Every single child was engaged in a conversation with an adult. "Here we are in a room full of people that they have never met before until an hour ago, yet look at them," I said, "They are conversing with people of different ages." She shook her head up and down without a word.

If I've been asked that question once, I've been asked it a hundred times. "What about socialization?" If a picture is worth a thousand words, then I have several hundred thousand words of proof that my children have had ample socialization, because I have purposely taken lots of pictures. Home schooling does not mean we stay home all day with the windows closed and the doors shut. Home schooling does not mean that we never speak to people or only associate with our own kind. Home schooling allows us to be fully integrated into society where we are interacting with a variety of people at various ages.

The Middle Years

One of our most unusual socialization experiences came on a day when our home school support group met at Shawnee Park in Xenia, Ohio. Our county was hosting a weeklong all day summer camp at that same location. Another home schooler had enrolled her children in the day camp and told us about it. I decided to take our children and check it out. Since the day camp was for older children and it started an hour before the support group park day, I decided to stay around and play with our two younger sons, Matthew and Micah.

I took five-year-old Matthew and two-year-old Micah over to the swing set, slide and jungle gym to play. I was close enough to see the camp activities. Our newly turned fourteen-year-old Michael sat on the picnic table near the day campers and watched as the college-aged camp directors assembled and readied them for games. Before long they invited him to participate along with his twelve-year-old brother Mark and ten-year-old twin sisters, Jennifer and Janet.

Thirty-five children were there from the community. My children did not know any of them except for the other two home schoolers. After an hour had past, I glanced over to see our two oldest boys fully involved in the camp games. In fact, they were so involved in their play with the children, that the camp directors felt comfortable enough to go sit by the side of the trailer. They were busy talking and getting ready for the next activity.

By the second hour, while Matthew and Micah and I were eating lunch with the support group, Michael and Mark were dividing the children into two groups. Michael, the fourteen-year-old, led one group of fifteen children in forming alphabets with their bodies to spell words, while Mark led the other. The girls were following along. The three camp directors were now sitting on a hill nearby, watching.

By the third hour, one of three camp directors approached me to compliment me on my children's behavior. She shared her initial concern when she saw me walk up with six children. At one point, five-year-old Matthew (Mr. Sociable himself) came over to speak with her. Now, she was so impressed with the boys taking charge that she asked if they could come work for the rest of the week and the next month at a different location. She even gave them each a volunteer T-shirt with the county logo that very same day. What a blessed mother I was! I smiled as I looked around and pondered, "Where are all those people who wonder about socialization?"

The Families of Knollwood Home Support Group visit The U.S. Capitol

One of our many Social Get-togethers

PEACH gets involved in the community Old Fashion Days' Parade

The Ulmer, Denen, Sutton, and Cross Family visit Caprine Estates

A local goat farm

The Older Years

It was a quarter until five in the evening. "*Great!*" I thought, *we'll have just enough time to grab a bite to eat before Michael and Mark go on duty at Burger King.* A local Burger King was supportive of the community by allowing various groups to come in and collect customer receipts as a fundraiser in exchange for a few hours of work. Our sons were on a community select soccer team that needed money for uniforms and equipment. Since all the children were with me, I decided to make it our place for dinner that night. The twins, twelve-year-olds, Jennifer and Janet had gone on ahead with their younger brothers. They ordered and moved through the line. I ordered. Several people came in behind me to order. Next, Michael and Mark entered. They scanned the menu. Since the line had grown full so quickly, we were all waiting for our food. I looked down the line to see what was taking them so long to place their order and noticed the cashier engaged in more than just order taking but also a conversation with Michael and Mark.

There was a little mix up in my order, so while I continued to wait, the line of people now dwindled down to me. My order came, but Michael and Mark were still talking to the cashier. I moved closer to them and overheard her ask, "Where do you go to school?" "We're home schooled," they said. "Did you know we're hiring at 15?" I joined the conversation at this point. "Did you say you're hiring at 15?" I asked, now noticing by her nametag that she was the store manager. "Are these your sons?" she asked. "Yes," I answered, not knowing what to expect next. "Well, they are sure well-mannered," she said, "I'd like for them to come work for me."

Later, in the car, I asked Michael and Mark if they knew why a store manager would ask them if they wanted a job, especially since she had never met them before. Neither answered. "Unfortunately," I said, "our society has become accustom to many teenagers being rude, disrespectful and irresponsible. When adults meet young people who address them properly and engages in intelligent conversation, it's rare."

I'm still amazed after all these years of home schooling that people continue to make socialization an issue. I wish we had captured on video camera all of the social experiences of our children. They are not hermits, weird or freaks. They are able to communicate socially with any age group. Opportunities for socialization for home schoolers abound.

However, to address this issue of socialization in their teen years for future references for colleges or jobs, I began to collect "Letters of Recommendations" from people with whom the boys interacted. If they played for a local community sports team, I asked the coach for a brief letter or the piano teacher or from folks for whom they did odd jobs. These were people who worked in our community as art museum docents, lawyers, nurses, engineers or military personnel. One neighbor was a nurse with her own home-based business. I requested the letter of recommendation be put on professional letterhead.

Socialization for our family included our involvement with church activities, the ministry to the homeless through the Gospel Mission of Dayton, and the building of homes through Habitat for Humanity in Xenia. Socialization also included our home school support group activities, park days, field trips, art lessons, ballet lessons, piano lessons, sports activities and visiting with other families. These were more than enough social experiences!

Socialization also came at other times. For example, Michael our seventeen-year-old taught piano lessons from our home for three years. He had fifteen students scheduled for lessons at thirty-minute increments. Often times, these mothers would bring along siblings. While the lesson went on, I visited with the mother and our children played.

There were other opportunities for social experiences during the time when my husband Michael headed up the F-117 office at Wright Patterson AFB and hosted yearly picnics for the office workers and neighborhood. These gatherings usually totaled at least one hundred co-workers plus their families. Our children received ample opportunity to be socialized.

Through the years, I have counseled with new home schoolers or moms who needed encouragement. They always brought along their children, so this made it possible for our children to visit too. We home churched in two different states at times and met several families. That meant our house had a revolving door with people in and out. Socialization? We rarely worried about socialization…

We found that any place we went became a social experience. Whether it was to the grocery store, the gas station, the post office, or the bank. Socialization need not be an issue. In fact, it's not. But that's very hard for those outside of home schooling to understand. So, be encouraged to take those photos of social moments and share them.

Chapter 13

How Do You Do It?

"Whatever you do, work at it with all your heart,
As working for the Lord, not for men,
Since you know that you will receive an inheritance
From the Lord as a reward."
Colossians 3:23,24

"Finally, be strong in the Lord and His mighty power. Put on the full armor of God so that you can take your stand against the devil's schemes. For our struggle is not against flesh and blood, but against the powers of authorities, against the powers of this dark world and against the spiritual forces of evil in the heavenly realms. Therefore, put on the full armor of God, so that when the day of evil comes, you may be able to stand your ground and after you have done everything, to stand. Stand firm then, with the belt of truth buckled around your waist, with the breastplate of righteousness in place, and with your feet fitted with the readiness that comes from the gospel of peace. In addition to all this, take up the shield of faith, with which you can extinguish all the flaming arrows of the evil one. Take the helmet of salvation and the sword of the Spirit, which is the Word of God. And pray in the Spirit on all occasions with all kinds of prayers and requests. With this in mind, be alert and always keep on praying for all the saints."
Ephesians 6:10-18

ow do you do it?" I was often asked when people found out we had six children and had been home schooling for many years. "I pray a lot!" I would usually answer with a jovial smile. Families can't home school long without realizing the need for help from a "higher power" much higher than themselves. We attributed all of our success in home schooling to much prayer and total dependence on God.

God promised in His Word to provide everything we needed for life. It was really true! Sometimes it was energy to get up in the morning. Sometimes it was energy to stay up late at night to complete an unfinished task, prepare the next days' meal, or check the children's work. On some days, it was energy to prepare for an upcoming field trip, an event, or to have friends over. There were times when God graciously let "all" the children sleep later in the morning and I found great comfort in an hour or two of solitude just moving about the house without an interruption to my task or thoughts. Or maybe the Lord would allow me to get an afternoon nap that would help to energize me for the rest of the day.

I discovered that while my children were awake, I was constantly in what I termed "React Time." I was reacting or responding to their needs. That happened all day long! I found it difficult to think during this time. So I termed another phrase "Think Time." This was when it was quiet, there were no interruptions, and my thoughts did not flow in disjointed patterns that resemble a patchwork quilt. I love the early mornings for "think time" because it was here where I could read and study my Bible, plan meals, make grocery lists, schedule activities or appointments for the day, month or year, browse through a catalog, pick up or organize something, fold clothes or throw in a load of laundry.

> *As wife and mother, I directed my focus on my relationship with God by seeking to serve and please Him, my husband, and my children. My aim was to make our home a sanctuary.*

One thing I found extremely helpful was my "Things To Do" list or "Needs" list. I could jot down those important things that needed to be accomplished. (There are many expensive planners on the market today, but the same results can be accomplished with your own home made sheet). I also found that jotting down my thoughts the night before or during the day for the next day helped to keep me on track. I learned to make a plan, work the plan and execute the plan. I learned to shop as if we were a small business. We made bulk purchases from places like Sam's Club and divided up the large portions into smaller ones. We were involved in a food co-op where we were able to obtain more healthy organic type items. These bulk purchases were very beneficial when shared amongst several families. For example, I could purchase a 50-pound bag of whole oats or other grains for fifteen dollars as opposed to a 16-ounce package of overly processed oatmeal for three dollars and get much more for our money. I learned how to prepare two and three meals at the same time. We would eat one and freeze the other two. After a few weeks of this habit, we would have a month of meals in the freezer. This was helpful because it kept me from running out to the stores as frequently.

Another timesaving idea I utilized was when I purchased a small postal scale to weigh my letters. I bought stamps by the roll of a hundred (stamps can now be purchased through ATM machines when you do your banking or ordered through the mail.) With the new computer technology, you can purchase your own software and mail packages with metered postage from home. I bought several cards for special events such as birthdays, get-well, sympathy cards ahead by ordering through a mail-order company. This can save time and eliminate last-minute frustration.

We learned to divide time one week at a time. We set aside Sunday as a day for worship, fellowship and rest. We utilized Sunday evenings for planning and sharing the upcoming week's events with the family. As wife, I directed my focus on my relationship with God by seeking to serve and please Him, my husband and my children. My aim was to make our home a sanctuary. It was a place where my husband could come to retreat from the difficulties of the world, a place where I could host neighbors or friends, and a place where our children would love to play and grow up.

I learned to appreciate my husband. He was not too proud to help clean the kitchen, wash a dish, put on a load of laundry, vacuum take the children out to play, or let me run out for a break. Many times this was after a hard day at work or when he had returned from a weeklong trip away. Sometimes he would give me words of encouragement or correction. I could never have done it without his support and help. I learned to consult with him before I committed to anything.

I learned to depend on the children, to enlist their help. This training was for their future responsibilities that life would bring. It made them feel needed, wanted, helpful and grown-up.

Every now and then, unexpected phones call or note in the mail from a friend that would "make my day." I considered these individuals to be in my "Amen Corner." They were the ones that said, "You can do it! Wow, you're amazing! Keep up the great work! You're doing a wonderful job! Thank for your help and encouragement!" Their encouragement on some days was just the boost I needed to help keep me going.

I learned to keep reading. I was not able to do this so much when the children were younger, but as they grew older, my reading time increased. I read helpful magazines or books that aided me in my "professional development" as a Christian, a mother, wife, educator and friend.

I found great support and encouragement from involvement in support groups. It was there that I found other women who could relate to my struggles. It was there that I gleaned from the wisdom and experience of others.

I learned to ask for help from the ladies in my church, neighbors, friends, or family members (when they were in town).

I learned to plan ahead. I did not wait until the end of the year or until the summer but I planned throughout the year. I purchased needed books a few at a time or collected the name of curriculum I wanted to use for the upcoming year. I thought about the things our family desired to become involved in and tried to count the cost of that involvement in terms of time, energy, money and goal accomplishment.

I learned to keep a notebook and pen by my bed for those sparks of inspiration that the Holy Spirit gave. Sometimes it was an idea to resolve a learning difficulty, a conflict with a child, a creative teaching tip or ideas like this book to other home schoolers.

I learned to take one day at a time. Life can throw so many curve balls at you. I also learned to be flexible. Through the years, the only constant in our home school was change. The manner in which we prepared for that change or responded to that change made a big difference!

So how did I do it? "I prayed a lot!" In fact, looking back, my life became one long conversation with God. I simply prayed over everything. It was my way of teaching the children how to pray. We prayed as we left the driveway. We prayed over our purchases. We prayed as we put of the Whole Armor of God each day (remembering that we are soldiers in His army). We prayed for wisdom, for guidance, for directions, for help, and for friends.

The Cross Crew Working Together

Chapter 14

Discipleship: The Secret To Well Behaved Children

"I have no greater joy than to hear that my children are walking in the truth."
3 John 1:4

"Children, obey your parents in the Lord, for this is right.
'Honor your father and mother'
-Which is the first commandment with a promise—
That it may go well with you and that you may enjoy long life on the earth."
Ephesians 6:1

I t was 12:30 when the phone rang. "Hope I didn't interrupt your school time," the voice on the other end apologized. I didn't mind because I was sitting under my shady maple tree at the picnic table enjoying temporary tranquility. In fact, I was staring into my gathering basket filled with the tail end of the summer's garden. Thankfulness welled inside me to see the bright red cherry tomatoes, okra, dried marigolds, jalapeno peppers, straw flowers, and lavender. The fresh scent of the just cut lavender coupled with the gentle cool breeze had a rather soothing effect. Janet, my ten-year-old, was playing on the swing set with her younger two brothers. Jennifer, her twin, was in her room working on Math. Mark, my twelve-year-old had taken it upon himself to patch an 18 by 18 inch section of drywall in the garage that the dog had gnawed out. I could hear his happy whistles and the buzzing of the drill bit. Michael the fourteen-year-old had been on the phone earlier calling computer companies for answers to his questions. Everyone was happy. Everyone was content. The picture I paint in no way reflects the scene that had taken place earlier that morning. My expectations for the day were simple (or so I thought)- a worship time, clean-up/chores, academics, then play and other activities.

The worship and praise time soon turned into a war zone. Just as we were about to begin our sing time, Micah our two-year-old smeared breakfast all over himself, his high chair and the floor. He then proceeded to climb out and was attempting to crawl across the table. All this in less than 3 seconds! "OK, what song shall we sing this morning?" I asked while scooping Micah into my arms.

Matthew, my five-year-old, was in constant motion. First he was in his chair, and then he was out of it. "I don't want to sing!" Matthew stated emphatically as he pushed his cars and trucks across the kitchen table. Mark was holding a praise chorus book. He found a song that he liked and began to sing. Janet decided that there was a better one that matched the Ephesians text we were reading and she began to sing that one. "Don't do that, Janet!" Jennifer cried, but the chaos was building and everyone seemed oblivious to anyone else. Michael, our 14-year-old, had excused himself from the table and decided to wait on the family room sofa (in the reclining position) while the commotion passed. My frustration was building. "Please don't let Satan distract us!" I pleaded. "But Mommy! I just can't concentrate with all this noise," Michael said. The tears began to roll down my cheeks. I closed my Bible and turned to go up the stairs. I locked myself in the bathroom and began to pray, "Lord, you know I desire to do what is right. I'm doing my best and I don't understand why there is all of this turmoil. Please help me!"

I took a few minutes to compose myself and started back down the stairs only to be met by my wide-eyed children. "What's the matter, Mommy?" they asked. "Children, Mommy and Daddy love you. We only want the best for you and it's frustrating when you don't listen. This is our worship time to give honor to God. We are studying to show ourselves approved as workman who do not need to be ashamed, but who correctly handle the word of truth." (Sermon # 56 in the Motherhood Series) I was then able to correct each child and go on with our praise time. Remember, the goal of home education is to "Train a child in the way he should go…" (Proverbs 22:6) Training takes time, lots and lots of time, and lots and lots of energy! So…be patient.

> Discipleship is a life-long process. Each individual was has a personal relationship with the Lord Jesus Christ will progress at a different rate through out his or her lifetime on earth.

It is also extremely important to introduce them to God's plan of salvation in Jesus Christ. A wonderful foundation of Bible doctrines to can be taught to very young children as you "walk along the way, rise up and sit down." Over time, they can be taught about His creation, His Word, His plan to redeem mankind through His Son, Jesus, His power, comfort, and guidance for us here on earth by His Holy Spirit. They can be taught about our enemy-Satan, and about our defense-the Whole Armor of God (Ephesians 6:10-18). A child who comes to know Jesus as their personal Lord and Savior answers to a higher call than father, mother and the rod of correction. This child will want to please God. This is why discipleship is so important. Correct doctrine must be taught. As father opens the Word of God daily and reads to his children and mother nurtures, cares for, and teaches the children daily, home becomes the training ground for service to the Lord. That service begins immediately upon their accepting Jesus! Do not squelch the Spirit within them. Do not tell them when they grow up they can serve Him; teach them how to walk and live God's will everyday now! Live the Christian life before them, everyday. Share Christ love everywhere you go and in every way, every single day! If your family does that, your lights will so shine before men that those who see, will glorify your Father in heaven.

There is also some practical advice that I would give to aid with helping children to behave, that comes with understanding them. At times, you must view life from their perspective. Children love to play, and they love to have fun. So don't make home schooling all work and no play. Our family worked hard together and we played hard together. We always sat down with them before we went various places to forewarn them of where we were going, what we were going to do there, and our expectations for their behavior. We stated the consequences for misbehavior and then followed through on the discipline. Sometimes this was very inconvenient. We told them that they represented our family, the Lord Jesus Christ, our church and our community. Whenever we traveled, we made sure they were well fed, clean and pottied. Often I carried a gallon of water, cups, and a porta-potty in the car. If we were to be gone during a meal, I prepared something for them to eat. When they were younger, they seemed to want to eat earlier and more often. So adjust for your family. Prepare an activity bag for the car. You can keep coloring books, story books with good character training, crayons, markers, etc. for those times when you are out and about with errands and the children can keep busy with their hands and minds.

Discipleship is a life-long process. Each individual who has a personal relationship with the Lord Jesus Christ will progress at a different rate through out his or her lifetime on earth. We as parents do not and cannot control our children's relationship with the Lord. We can model it before them and point the way to Him. The Spirit of the Living God does it all.

Chapter 15

What Role Does Dad Play?

"O my people, hear my teaching; listen to the words of my mouth. I will open my mouth in parables, I will utter Hidden things, things from of old- what we have heard and known, what our fathers have told us. We will not hide them from their children; we will tell the next generation the praiseworthy deeds of the Lord, his power, and the Wonders he has done. He decreed statutes for Jacob and established the law in Israel, which he commanded our Forefathers to teach their children, so the next generation would know them, even the children yet to be born, and they in turn would tell their children. Then they would put their trust in God and would not forget his deeds but would keep his commands. They would not be like their forefathers - a stubborn and rebellious generation, whose Hearts were not loyal to God, whose spirits were not faithful to him."
Psalm 78:1-8

"Listen, my sons, to a father's instruction; pay attention and gain understanding. I give you sound learning; so do Not forsake my teaching. When I was a boy in my father's house, still tender, and an only child of my mother, he taught me and said, lay hold of my words with all your heart; keep my commands and you will live."
Proverbs 4:1-4

he officers of our support group were invited to a couple's dinner. "Just keep the teacher happy!" I overheard my husband say to one of the other home schooling fathers. He was smiling so I stepped over a little closer. "What's so funny?" I asked. "Oh, he was just giving me a little advice between us Dads," Ed said.

Several months later, I was planning an article for our Parents Educating At Christian Homes newsletter entitled, "How Do You Spell Relief?" The answers given by the ladies varied but there was one answer that came across loud and clear. Here's how they spelled relief:

Diane Cope S-U-M-M-E-R

Becky Francis D-A-D

Sandy Sjoquist D-A-D

Margaret Degler H-O-T B-A-T-H (Lots of Bubbles)

Annette Fideler P-R-A-Y-E-R /E-A-T-I-N-G O-U-T

Yvonne Hesler P-R-A-Y-E-R (going in the yard and screaming)

Lisa Halsey D-A-D-D-Y

Gilda Winkler J-E-S-U-S/Dr. Dobson's Calendar

Cathy Johnson T-H-E L-O-R-D (Phil. 1:6)

Laurie Blair D-A-D's H-O-M-E

Notice how several of the ladies said "D-A-D." I cannot stress or over emphasize the importance of Dad's role enough. Training is the God-given responsibility of Dad-the Father, Son of Adam-Man, though he may delegate some responsibilities to his wife. God will hold him accountable for this gift of family he has been given. Below is a list of "musts":

---

1. He must have a personal relationship with the Lord Jesus Christ. A man will never fully understand his purpose here on earth without knowing the plan of God.

2. He is a priest before his family; he is responsible for teaching and training them in spiritual matters. He is the watchman, guarding over them. This cannot be overemphasized enough. He must pray for them. He must! He must! He must! Why? The wife and mother who chooses to stay home is on the front lines of the battleground. Satan wants nothing more than to destroy the family. Particularly, he would love to destroy your family, your marriage, your children, or your testimony. The enemy will come against the mother and children in the home in many ways. He (Satan) will also come against the father in many other ways. Stay in the Word and in prayer!

3. He must recognize the spiritual oneness with his wife. Chapter 5:1,2 of Genesis says "When God created man, he made him in the likeness of God. He created them male and female and blessed them. And when they were created, he called them 'man'. "Chapter 5:22-33 of Ephesians tells us "Husbands ought to love their wives as their own bodies;" "He must love his wife as he loves himself." From God's perspective, the two (husband and wife) are one. This marital union with Christ as the Head, blesses his family. God will use the family to minister to those in the neighborhood, in the workplace, at church and possibly around the world.

---

4. He is a role model and should lead by example. Therefore, he must be a man of character. He should possess the traits of integrity, truthfulness, honesty, trustworthiness, compassion, contentment, courage, decisiveness, dependability, determination, diligence, discernment, discretion, empathy, enthusiasm, faithfulness, generosity, gentleness, kindness, humility, initiative, joyfulness, loyalty, obedience, patience, purity, responsibility, self-control, tenderheartedness, and thankfulness.

5. He must manage his household well. He must make sure the basic needs of his family are met: shelter, clothing, food, finances, furniture, equipment, and materials. A man who learns to lead in the home will be a man able to lead in the church, the body of Christ. I Timothy 3:1-13 lays down the qualifications "a deacon must be the husband of but one wife and must manage his children and his household well." Gentlemen, this is your training ground. Lessons learned here can benefit you in every area outside of the home.

6. He must learn to be a good listener. A woman with children all day has a lot to share!

7. He must assist in making the home an orderly, worshipful, lovely, peaceful place to dwell. Jointly make decisions about decorating the home and maintaining the home on a realistic budget. Physically work together to hang the curtains, repair, rebuild or restore the home.

8. He must learn to be a better teacher because he is one. God will allow you time to learn as you teach and train your children.

9. He must be the spiritual leader. Reading God's Word, seeking godly mentors, disciplining others with what you have learned and worshiping with other believers will aid you in becoming that leader.

10. He must love his children. You, their earthly father, represent God the Heavenly Father. Show tenderness and compassion. Didn't Jesus show tenderness and compassion to you? You must hug your children. Bear hugs are great, but tender ones can teach how a big strong man controls great power within himself. Express care, concern and affection to your children. Doesn't the Bible teach, "Whoever claims to live in Him must walk as Jesus did?"

11. He must work hard and teach his family to work. The curse due to the fall of Adam was "Man shall toil the soil." Yes, we are under the new covenant and Jesus did die for all of our sins, but the consequences of sin are still valid. Man must toil the soil while here on earth.

Let's Get Personal-Practical Helps

- Husband, it is so important to keep the marriage bed undefiled. Ungodly television programs, magazines or movies must be eliminated. "There must not be even a hint of sexual immorality among you." (Ephesians 5:3) Your love and commitment for that one woman will protect you, strengthen you and glorify God. This woman is your lifelong helpmate, your dearest friend and the mother of your children.

- Husband, love your wife/be romantic with her. Each man must live with his wife in an understanding way. In plain English: gentlemen you must *know* your wife-her likes, her dislikes, her weaknesses, her failures, her strengths, her successes, her upbringing, her experiences, her dreams. You must take the initiative and find as many ways as you can to express love to her. You must learn her language of love. Occasionally, surprise her by coming home fifteen to thirty minutes early. Occasionally bring her home a meaningful gift-a magnet with carefully chosen words from *you*, a special book she may need or want, a scented candle reserved for your times together, a shower gel or bottle of lotion to massage away the stress of the day or her favorite fast food meal.

- Husband, verbally praise and encourage your wife. Please do not take her for granted. Do not fall into the trap of thinking *it's her job, not mine!* Try it for a weekend or two every month. This experience will provide you with the necessary insight into each child and their character. Also, it will give you an appreciation for the job your wife does in the home. Remember she functions by the way God designed her-out of her love and dedication to the Lord, her love for you-her husband and her commitment to her children.

- Husband, provide your wife with days off. In a regular job, seven to fourteen days per year are allotted to sick leave or vacation time. She deserves a time of refreshment and rejuvenation. You will be blessed and the children will be blessed also!

- Husband, participate as often as possible in support group activities such as monthly meetings, field trips, or yearly state conventions. This is a great opportunity to meet other Dad's and see families like your own, in action.

- Husband, expose your wife to your world, your job, your fears, your hurts and your struggles. Gentlemen, that means communicate. "Fine," is not a complete sentence, nor does it tell her anything. It is possible to give descriptions about your work world without compromising information or gossiping about people. It is helpful to give your wife a list of things in your work world that she can pray about. This helps her to focus on your specific needs and helps her to know how to pray for you throughout the day. It is helpful to have a daily prayer time together and time when you both coordinate the activities of the day (we review the weekly schedule on Sunday evening and then again each morning). This helps to keep you both on the same sheet of music. Bring your wife and family into the office once a year or so. Let them see what challenges you face and what your life is like while they are at home. Share, share, share, this will draw you together as a couple.

- Pray together daily—before you leave for work and at night before bed.

- Read books together. It is important to have common topics you can discuss and share.

- Take her on marriage retreats.

Other Practical Helps:	
Get into the Word of God	Bible teacher
Develop a vision for your family	Teach as he goes
Jointly dream and plan with your wife	Lover/friend
Communicate clearly with your wife and children	Disciplinarian
Meet with other men for Bible study/accountability	Transparent
Coach wife and children	Overseer/principal
Physical education instructor	Coach/counselor
Keep the Big Picture!	Visionary
Know where you trying to go with each child.	Family philosophy
Meet with other men for Bible study/accountability	
Coach wife & coach children	

The Husbands/Fathers of the Knollwood Home School Support Group

A Father

By Mrs. Eula V. Ware

A father is sent by God to lead his family and teach them what is right.

A father guides his family by day and by night.

A father loves his family and protects them from harm.

A father is a charm.

For the mother, he is her husband and her lover.

For the children, he is greater than any other.

He works hard for his family; he would not have it any other way.

We give thanks to God everyday for the man that lets the Lord guide his way.

He is worth much more than the material things he provides.

It is his love for his family deep inside that his family loves him dearly.

They know they are blessed.

When you have a man of God as a father,

You have the best!

A father to your family is simply God's request.

"Through your offspring all peoples on earth will be blessed."

Acts 3:25

Chapter 16

Mothering is A Profession

"As apostles of Christ we could have been a burden to you, but we were gentle among you, like a mother caring for Her little children."
I Thessalonians. 2:7

"Listen my son, to your father's instruction and do not forsake your mother's teaching."
Proverbs 1:8

"Charm is deceptive, and beauty is fleeting,
But a woman who fears the Lord is to be praised."
Proverbs 31:30

I completed a medical appointment at the military base and was on the highway headed home when I saw the next exit sign. For some strange reason, I was having my own private war inside as I tried to decide if I should exit and go to the local Kinko's for copies or just go on home. I decided to take advantage of my little outing since Jennifer and Janet were home watching the boys and drove over to the copy place. I entered the building and purchased my copy card. While some of my copies where printing, I decided to cut out one of the handouts. I noticed a gentleman nearby copying and cutting pages out of the Webster Dictionary. Since his pile was much higher than mine, I asked him if I might briefly use the scissors. "Of course," he said. We began to converse and he asked if I were a teacher at Wright State, just across the street. "No," I matter-of-factly stated, "I'm just a mother." "No," he replied gently, "I know you're much more than that." Normally, I was proud of my position as mother and I would spout off thirty thousand jobs that I attended to with the mother title but for some reason that particular day, I simply added, "I am a home educator and have been teaching my children at home for the last twelve years." His ears perked up when I made that statement and he invited me to come speak to the parents of his Upward Bound program. He took a few minutes to describe the program and it sounded interesting to me. Never wanting to miss an opportunity to answer God's invitation to share, I agreed to speak to the youths and parents of the Upward Bound program meeting on the campus of Central State University. This invitation came from Dr. Joseph Lewis, a well-known professor on campus. He also invited me to speak a second time, this time it was to an auditorium full of college students. Lastly, he invited me to speak in Dayton before a group of parents. Over the next year, I spoke to various groups. I led seminars on home education. I planned retreats for home schooling moms. I counseled women and college students. I was a test coordinator. I was a teacher to my children. I felt like a professional!

I didn't get that feeling of professionalism after washing the dishes for the umpteenth time or folding the laundry or mopping the floor or refereeing an argument between the children. There have been times, when as a mother in the home, I felt less than or inferior to other women who held jobs and earned money. But there were also times when I felt especially blessed with the opportunity to be able to stay home and accomplish those things, which were important to our family and our home running smoothly. God always reminded me-as I delved into His Word that I was a professional with an incredible job! He had given me an awesome responsibility when he made me a woman. It would be my lifelong task to live up to the title.

This especially hit home one morning about 4 a. m. when Michael, my husband, came to sit down on the side of the bed before he dashed off to work. He was retired from the military and in a civilian job that depended on contracts for income. On this particular morning he wasn't moving too fast. He was just sitting there with his shoulders hung down, not speaking. I lifted my head off the pillow and sat up. As sleepy and tired as I was, I realized what my job as helpmate required. I put my arms around him, massaged his neck and shoulders, and began to pray for him. When I finished praying, he shared with me the status of his current crisis, a few other difficulties, and a number of issues that were plaguing him. Now I knew exactly how to pray for him throughout that day. "A wife of noble character, who can find? She is worth far more than rubies. Her husband has full confidence in her and lacks nothing of value. She brings him good, not harm, all the days of her life…" (Proverbs 31:10-12)

After Michael left for work, I went into the bathroom to pick up the dirty towels, clothes, and socks left from that morning and to clean the mess the children made the night before. It was 5:30 a. m. and quiet, and I loved working in peace. I came out and stared into my closet that definitely needed a cleaning. *That will have to wait*, I thought. In fact, I decided it was time to hire my daughters or sons to do a job I didn't have time to do anymore. I labeled three bags: give away; throw away; and keep. It was a great organizing technique that I learned from Emilie Barnes years ago. I did what I could to sort, then moved to the bed and placed the comforter back in place.

I mentally ran through a list of possible ideas for Michael's upcoming birthday. I needed to finish up with gift purchases and the surprise we had planned for him. Later that day, I made a quick call to his office secretary. My morning also included preparing for Bible study. I went downstairs and worked on a lesson from the Bible study I was co- leading with a friend. I loved the fact that the Holy Spirit was the teacher and we were earthen vessels, placed here to do His will. I simply needed to empty myself of all the anxieties of this world and renew my mind in His Word. I jotted notes of encouragement to the ladies who missed the class and to those who needed a human touch of God's love. I prayed for each woman and her specific situation. I prayed again for my husband and our children. Our oldest son Michael was down in Texas, going to school and working. He was transitioning into adulthood, and our relationship was not where we wanted it to be. Our second son Mark was attending a military prep school in Colorado. He was facing many challenges in his world. Others students who chose to break the rules were making it difficult for the entire group. Our twin daughters, Jennifer and Janet, were taking classes from a local secular community college; they too were facing challenges they had never faced before. Young men would call out to them as they walked down the corridors or teachers would present material the girls knew was in error. While they were thrilled at the great opportunity to be a witness and share their faith, it still required them to be on their constant guard. Our two younger sons, Matthew and Micah were still being home schooled. It was a tremendous daily challenge with their Attention Deficit Disorder and hyperactivity. We all needed prayer.

After finishing time in the Word, worshipping and laying my request before Him, I made a list of grocery items and other needs from the store and from a food co-op to which I belonged. I was planning ahead for the holidays, so I began to gather items for family gifts and a holiday get-together.

While calling our bank for a quick update of the funds in our account, I noticed some bills stacked on the desk, I wrote out the checks for the ones due. Hearing the boys starting to stir upstairs, I moved to the kitchen to mentally prepare for when they came down. I mentally prepared myself. *O.K. now smile, be loving and kind…* I told myself and started to sing "This is the day; this is the day that the Lord has made." I always purposed to brighten the start of each day, since it never made sense to me why anyone should wake up grouchy! I gave them each a hug as they came down the stairs and gave them a quick rundown of the day's assignments. "She selects wool and flax and works with eager hands. She is like the merchant ships, bringing her food for her family and portions for her servant girls. She considers a field and buys it; out of her earnings she plants a vineyard. She sets about her work vigorously; her arms are strong for her tasks. She sees that her trading is profitable, and her lamp does not go out at night." (Proverbs 31:13-18)

Micah went upstairs after breakfast and came back down with a pair of pants to be stitched. He had split them right in the middle. I glanced back over at the table. *I don't have time to do that right now,* I thought, *I need to finish packing and wrapping the shoe boxes of special gifts that our class had put together for Operation Christmas Child.* These boxes needed to be sent weeks ahead in order for them to be delivered by Christmas. I needed to finish gathering items for gift bags for the elderly in an independent retirement home that we frequently visited. "Pleeeease Mommy," Micah pleaded.

My stomach was starting to grumble, so I juiced some carrots into an eight-ounce glass. I decided to take my vitamins and minerals at the same time. My battle of the bulge was just that, a battle! I fought with my fleshly desires; so I sat down to make a grocery list of better food options when we were hungry. We needed more fresh vegetables, more beans, and more whole grains. "She opens her arms to the poor and extends her hands to the needy. When it snows, she has no fear for her household; for all of them are clothed in scarlet. She makes coverings for her bed; she is clothed in fine linen and purple. Her husband is respected at the city gate, where he takes his seat among the elders of the land. She makes linen garments and sells them, and supplies the merchants with sashes. She is clothed with strength and dignity; she can laugh at the days to come. She speaks with wisdom, and faithful instruction is on her tongue. She watches over the affairs of her household and does not eat the bread of idleness." (Proverbs 31:20-27)

I received a card in the mail. It was from our second son Mark. He was nineteen and waking up to the realities of the world around him. It read "Thank you Mom & Dad for all the things you've done for me. From changing my diaper to…" What a blessing! Thank you Lord! I went upstairs and bent down to pick up an envelope that had fallen off the little table near our bed. I opened it to find an old card from my husband Michael. "To my dearest, best-est and only friend! Thank you for loving me." I looked in the mirror. My cheeks were beginning to sag. The number of gray hairs was increasing in the midst of the brownish blonde ones. "Her children arise and call her blessed; her husband also, and he praises her: Many women do noble things, but you surpass them all." (Proverbs 31:28,29)

The home schooling mother is multi-talented. She is a theologian as she studies God's word to understand it and teach it. She is a scientist as she studies, observes, and collects data on her world, her husband, and her children. She is a science teacher when she does experiments with them. She is a politician as she keeps abreast of the current issues in local, state and federal government. She is an art teacher as she does crafts and projects. She is a mathematics teacher. She is the physical education instructor. She is referee of all games and arguments. She is field trip coordinator as she arranges and schedules field trips to coordinate with their studies. She is a home executive as she manages the home with record keeping, bills, food, clothing and supply management. She is both the doctor and nurse when the temperature rises and she prescribes chicken broth, Tylenol, lots of rest and hugs. She is the nutritionist as she shops for the best foods for her family. She is principal, teacher, assistant, bookkeeper, accountant, maid, cook, laundry attendant, guidance counselor, marriage and family counselor, and the UPS and postal service. She is her husband's helpmate. She is the lover of her husband. She is her children's advocate. "Charm is deceptive, and beauty is fleeting; but a woman who fears the Lord is to be praised. Give her the reward she has earned, and let her works bring her praise at the city gate." (Proverbs 31:30,31) This profession of motherhood is a job learned through the daily grind of life. It is a job that each woman will grow into over the span of time. With each passing moment and experience, she will glean knowledge about many topics and learn about her own relationship with the Lord.

I would like to share some of my insights about a woman's purpose gleaned from the scriptures as I looked at the beginning and the end of a woman's life. In the beginning, Adam and Eve sinned against God. To Eve, God said "I will greatly increase your pains in childbearing; with pain you will give birth to children. Your desire will be for your husband,

and he will rule over you." (Genesis 3:16) If Eve is the mother of all living then we are following in her footsteps. Her first purpose was to be that of a helpmate to her husband. It was her job to complete him. Next, we see that together they are to procreate. She will bear the children.

From the book of Proverbs, chapter 31, we are given a glimpse of a truly virtuous woman. She is a gift from God to her husband. From the book of Timothy, it says, "A woman should learn in quietness and full submission. I do not permit a woman to teach or to have authority over a man; she must be silent. For Adam was formed first, then Eve. And Adam was not the one deceived; it was the woman who was deceived and became a sinner. But women will be saved through childbearing- if they continue in faith, love and holiness with propriety." (I Tim. 2:11-15) Now just what does that mean? We know that women are saved through Christ and Christ alone. After home schooling for lo these many years, living through my own upbringing in a large family of thirteen children, watching my mother and other women through the years, and examining the women in the Bible, I view this verse through different eyes. I see the God-given task of a woman through the mothering process, as one vital and important way God will teach her about Himself. As she parents, according to the Scriptures, she will be drawn deeper into fellowship with God. She will come to know sorrow, hurt, pain and the power of prayer. These will help her to identify with Christ and his sufferings. She will grow in her faith, trust and belief. She will deepen and expand her definition of love. She will seek holiness, desire peace and the satisfaction of her soul.

> # A woman stands at a very strategic place as wife and mother in the home. She is a gatekeeper. She is a watchman. Her ministry will touch the world…

From the book of Titus, we find him charging the older women "likewise, teach the older women to be reverent in the way they live, not to be slanderers or addicted to much wine, but to teach what is good. Then they can train the younger women to love their husbands and children, to be self-controlled and pure, to be busy at home, to be kind, and to be subject to their husbands, so that no one will malign the word of God." (Titus 2:3-5) I truly believe that simply giving birth does not make you a mother. Oh no! A mother is much, much more.

There are jewels for us women to be found in the passages concerning the day the baby Jesus was taken to the temple to be circumcised. There was a man called Simeon who was righteous and devout, waiting for the consolation of Israel. There was also a prophetess, Anna, the daughter of Phanuel, of the tribe of Asher. She was very old. She had lived with her husband seven years after her marriage, and then was a widow until she was eighty-four. She never left the temple but worshipped night and day, fasting and praying. Coming up to them (Joseph, Mary & Jesus) at that very moment, she gave thanks to God and spoke about the child to all who were looking forward to the redemption of Jerusalem." (Luke 2:36-38) Our clue: She worshipped day and night, fasting and praying in the temple. Both she and Simeon were waiting with expectancy!

Another wisdom passage for us women is found in I Timothy, "Give proper recognition to those widows who are really in need. But if a widow has children or grandchildren, these should learn first of all to put their religion into practice by caring for their parents and grandparents, for this is pleasing to God. The widow who is really in need and left all alone puts her hope in God and continues night and day to pray and to ask God for help..." (I Tim. 4:3-5) "No widow may be put on the list of widows, unless she is over sixty, has been faithful to her husband, and is well known for her good deeds, such as bringing up children, showing hospitality, washing the feet of the saints, helping those in trouble and devoting herself to all kinds of good deeds." (I Tim. 4:9,10) Our clues: Widows were "fasting and praying." They were known for their "good deeds." They were "bringing up children, showing hospitality, washing the feet of the saints, helping those in trouble and devoting herself to all kinds of good deeds."

Earl and Diane Rodd in their booklet entitled "Dealing With Anger," states these purposes for why the mother is in the home:

#1 The mother is in the home school situation to learn godly patience. The Lord doesn't want His daughter to act on impulse or to be driven by outward circumstances (e.g. a child's disobedient behavior). He wants the mother to learn how to be:

a. Quick to hear the Holy Spirit and obey His Word.

b. Slow to speak her own words.

c.   Slow to vent her own emotions or her own anger.

#2 The mother is in the home school situation to learn spiritual warfare. A mother must realize that she and her child have an enemy whole sole purpose is to steal their relationship of love and unity and to kill any testimony that the Lord's Word is true.

A woman stands at a very strategic place as wife and mother in the home. She is a gatekeeper. She is a watchman. Her ministry will touch the world as her children grow up, leave home and impact it in some way. She can look behind her in the past to see the path she has taken. She can assess where this path led her. She can glean from her mistakes and build on her successes. She can train, introduce and build into her children good character qualities learned. She can glean from her husband's upbringing and glean from his mistakes and build on his successes. She can purposely introduce, train and build into their children strength of character. She can look to the future to what type of adult she would like to have a part in producing in accordance with God's divine creation of this child. Her greatest gift, tool, task will be the instrument of prayer. She must utilize it often for her husband, her children, herself and for others.

"But women will be saved through childbearing —if they continue in faith, love, and holiness with propriety." I Timothy 2:15

Nancy Cook & Michelle Roebuck   *Jacqueline, Sharon Thompson, Susan Borm*

Jacqueline, Sharon McKeever   *Jacqueline (Gilda) Winkler*

The Warrior

Author unknown

This morning my thoughts traveled along

To a place in my life where days have long since gone

Beholding an image of what I used to be

As visions were stirred, and God spoke to me

He showed me a Warrior, a soldier in place

Positioned by Heaven, yet I saw not the face

I watched as the Warrior fought enemies

This came from the darkness with destruction for me

I saw as the Warrior would dry away tears

As all of Heaven's Angels hovered so near

I saw many wounds on the Warrior's face

Yet weapons of warfare were firmly in place

I felt my heart weeping, my eyes held so much

As God let me feel the Warrior's prayer touched

I thought "how familiar" the words that were prayed

The prayers were like lighting that never would fade

I said to God "please, the Warrior's name"

He gave me no reply, He chose to refrain. I asked,

"Lord, who is broken that they need such prayer?"

He showed me an image of myself standing there

Bound by confusion, lost and alone

I felt prayers of the Warrior carry me home

I asked, "Please show me Lord, this Warrior so true"

I watched and I wept, for Mother…

The Warrior-was you!

Chapter 17

What About the Cost?

"Wisdom is supreme; therefore get wisdom.
Though it cost all you have, get understanding."
Proverbs 4:7

"Suppose one of you wants to build a tower.
Will he not first sit down and estimate the cost to see if he has enough money to complete it? For if he lays the
foundation and is not able to finish it, everyone who sees it will ridicule him, saying, 'This fellow began to
build and was not able to finish.'
...In the same way, any of you who does not give up everything he has cannot be my disciple."
Luke 14:28-30,33

I fell across the bed too exhausted to move. I glanced over at the clock; it was nearly one in the afternoon. "How am I ever going to make it through this day?" I asked myself. I remembered the lunch particles of bread, popcorn and spilled juice that lay underneath the bar stools of the kitchen counter. It was then that I heard commotion downstairs, and I knew my five-minute rest was over. *I don't have time to lie here*, I thought, *there's just too much work to do.*

This was one of the hardest chapters for me to write. I could not simply provide a list of materials, resources, and organizations without addressing the tremendous cost of home schooling in terms of the spiritual, physical, and emotional cost.

There is no job in the world that Michael and I found we worked harder at than our family. The fatigue of dealing with children all day long, especially in the young years is part of the cost.

After Michael had been hard at work all-day, flying, briefing other flyers, or just coming in off of a trip to another country or city, he wanted to come home and just relax. After I had been with the children all day or for weeks at a time, all I wanted was relief from the pressure. Now every day didn't work like that, but there were enough days that did go that way to make it part of the cost. Michael & I made it through these times because 1) we loved each other deeply 2) we loved our children very much and 3) we were committed to discipling our children to a personal relationship in Christ and maturity for adulthood. (See the Chapter called The Love Triangle)

Michael had to determine in his mind that the moment he stepped out of the car from work, it was family time. He usually came straight home, changed his clothes and went out to kick the ball around with the children. Usually this fun activity attracted the neighbor children so it provided an opportunity for him to be a Dad and a witness to children whose Dad's were unable. That meant that sometimes we had company for dinner. It was part of the cost to feed extra mouths. As the children grew older, he took them out to do yard work or change the oil in the car or take a ride to the hardware store or complete a project around the house. This provided me with just enough of a break to complete the dinner or take a quick shower or work on a project that had beckoned me all day. I had to determine that when the children were awake, it was their time, but when they were asleep, it was my time. This relieved me of the anxiety that I felt at times when "I" wanted to do something and felt like they were getting in the way. There were times when I had to completely give up on things like crafty projects that were time consuming and not beneficial. It was part of the cost of home schooling.

Then there is the time pressure of managing the marriage. When the children were young, we simply could not afford to go out weekly and pay for a babysitter too. So we found other ways. We counted office parties, dinner invites or church seminars as our dates. We creatively used every opportunity we could get away together to count as a date. Though we were in a room full of people, it was our date, and we were together. God also provided other couples along our home schooling pilgrimage who had children our ages. As our friendships developed and we trusted one another, we could swap babysitting for a day, overnighter or a weekend. It was part of the cost.

The cost of teaching the children was not only limited to the purchase of books and curriculum but there was a cost involved in attending seminars and conventions to learn about the variety of teaching materials available. There is also the emotional cost of trying to divide yourself amongst several children and feeling as though you're not meeting anyone's needs.

There is the cost of the home and equipment: the rooms that need to be picked up; the vacuuming that needs to get done; the furniture that needs to be dusted; the family room; the basement; the laundry; the bathrooms; the refrigerator that needs to be cleaned; the stove top that needs to be scrubbed; the trash that needs to be emptied; the garage that needs to be picked up and organized; the yard work; the photos; the bills; the notes to friends; the Christmas letter; the car registration; the checkbook; the grocery shopping. I'm sure I left a few items off of this never-ending list of home management. Even if you do not home school, these jobs in the home still have to be done, but with home schooling, they must be accomplished much more frequently.

> **The cost of home educating is enormous, tremendous, and sacrificial. Frankly, it will cost you and your spouse your lives. It will require a total giving of self to serve.**

Then there are the decisions about which activities to be involved in outside of the home. Should we attend the Sunday morning, Sunday night, Wednesday night, Friday night, Saturday night church programs? Do we allow the children to play on the community soccer, football, baseball, swim team or be involved in the local Christian school or start our own home school team? What about the art lessons, math tutor, piano lessons, college classes? All of these activities are part of the cost in terms of money and in terms of energy and let's not forget about the cost of gas for the car to run people all over the place.

Ah! Now we get to an overlooked area of the cost of home schooling. It is in the area of spiritual warfare that goes on as we seek to teach our children godly values. It takes time to get up and spend time in the presence of the Lord. It takes the presence of mind to be in prayer throughout the day for Daddy, the children, or the needs of others. It costs money to purchase study materials and uplifting books. Training the children in righteousness is an all day, minute- by-minute process that requires the mother to learn how to walk in the Spirit. The emotional roller coaster ride that we Moms sometimes find ourselves on is part of the cost. Fretting, worrying, and using words we don't mean are all a part of the cost.

The cost of home educating is enormous, tremendous, and sacrificial. Frankly, it will cost you and your spouse your lives. It will require a total giving up of self to serve. But if the goal is discipleship, then the payoffs will be worth it all. For the return on your eternal investment is incomprehensible. Dads and Moms, you will not know until we go to be with Him, the worth of your investment.

There have been many, many times when I wept and prayed, "Oh, God! I can't do this anymore!" There have been many times when I received phones calls of younger mothers saying "I can't do this anymore!" These were the times when I thought of those who had gone on before me. I thought of the thousands of home schoolers. I thought of my parents. I thought of their many years of faithful parent service to me and to my five sisters and seven brothers. After my father's retirement from the Army after 20 years, he took a job 150 miles away in another city for several years in order to provide for his family. Oh, the work! Oh, the struggle! I thought of Michael's parents and their sacrifice to go from one country to another for the sake of their family. For two years Michael and his younger sister and brother were left with relatives in Jamaica while his parents came over to the United States to make enough money to bring them over. Then I thought of my Lord. I thought of His suffering on that cross for me. Oh, the pain! Oh, the agony! Oh, the suffering he did for me! I thought of what it cost God to provide His One and only Son. And let's dare not leave out His Spirit who dwells in us, walks with us, comforts us and teaches us. What an investment in mankind!

> *There have been many, many times when I wept and prayed, "Oh God! I can't do this anymore!" ... The cost of home educating is enormous, tremendous, and sacrificial.*

Below are a few of the other costs of home schooling:

Home School Legal Defense Association $100 or $85 (if part of a large support group network)

Home Schooling Magazine Subscription $15 or more

Curriculum - Cost varies significantly

Supplies - Cost varies

Support Group $15-up

Field Trips- Museums, Gasoline, Lunches

Decisions/Maintenance:

Clothing/Shoes – Cost varies

Fatigue - Dealing with children all day.

Time pressures - Meals, management of the home and equipment, schoolwork,

Giving up for a season those things unnecessary for accomplishing the goal of home educating.

Can Mom home school, run a support group, teach Sunday school, coach baseball, soccer, and basketball? When is there time to volunteer for homeless shelter, prison ministry, etc. etc. etc.? What is the limit? Can a mother in the home be "all things to all people?" Can she hire a tutor or an older child to work with the younger children? Should she set aside quiet time for herself?

Chapter 18

When the Going Gets Tough

"I consider that our present sufferings are not worth comparing with the glory that will be revealed in us. The creation waits in eager expectation for the sons of God to be revealed. For the creation was subjected to frustration, not by its own choice, but by the will of the one who subjected it, in hope that the creation itself will be liberated from its bondage to decay and brought into the glorious freedom of the children of God. We know that the whole creation has been groaning as in the pains of childbirth right up to the present time. Not only so, but we ourselves, who have the first fruits of the Spirit, groan inwardly as we await eagerly for our adoption as sons, the redemption of our bodies. For in this hope we were saved. But hope that is seen is no hope at all. Who hopes for what he already has? But if we hope for what we do not yet have, we wait for it patiently. In the same way. The Spirit helps us in our weakness. We do not know what we ought to pray for, but the Spirit himself intercedes for us with groans that words cannot express. And He who searches our hearts knows the mind of the Spirit, because the Spirit intercedes for the saints in accordance with God's will."
Romans 8:18-26

"I have been driven many times to my knees by the overwhelming conviction
That I had nowhere else to go"
Abraham Lincoln

I called the children outside. We had just finished breakfast and it was time for our Bible Study. One by one they began arriving, and they stood there with a puzzled look on their faces. "Climb inside," I said as I held the handle to Matthew and Micah's little red wagon. "All of us?" Janet asked. "Yes," I replied. I was desperate for them to understand my point. They began to giggle and smirk about this silly exercise. While I held the handle, they crowded inside of the wagon, and I attempted to pull. It was heavy and difficult with all six of them in there. "Mom, you can't pull this wagon with all of us in here," and they began to the jump off. Now was the time for my teachable moment. "Children, when you were smaller, I could pull you in this wagon, but you're not little any more. I can't do everything. I can't get up early, make the breakfast, wash the clothes, clean the house, pay the bills, teach you children, shop for the groceries, keep up with the dental and doctor appointments, be a romantic wife, and stay up late preparing for the next day. I NEED YOUR HELP!

What happens when the going gets tough? The tough get praying! It's not the prayers have not already been going up, but this is a more intense, and deliberate focus on seeking His answers during these trying times. This is also a great time for evaluating the situation. It's time to assess and see where changes need to be made. Have you lost your way? Is it too confusing trying to figure out what to do first—the dirty dishes, the laundry, make the important phone call, help the child with math, or feed the baby? Is Dad into the job or in sin and neglecting the home, wife, or children? Is Mom so consumed with the children, home schooling, her responsibilities, or church activities that she's neglecting her husband or time in the Word? Are the uncontrollable circumstances of life pressing in?

As the number of children increase, so does the level of difficulty in sheer logistics-meals, clothing, appointments, Dad's needs, Mom's needs, the children's needs. This may be the time for a weekend retreat, where Dad and Mom evaluate what's going on and make the necessary adjustments. When the going gets tough, the tough get praying, planning and giving it over to God. I recall one of those tough times when I jotted a note to Sharon Thompson, my friend and fellow struggler:

> I feel like a drowning woman,
>
> floating in a great big sea.
>
> Every time a problem comes,
>
> The waves roll over me.
>
> I choke, I cough, I call to God
>
> "Help me not to drown
>
> In this sea of life surrounding me,
>
> Where the currents seem to pull
>
> me down..."

Refuse To Be Discouraged

Author unknown

I refuse to be discouraged, to be sad, or to cry;

I refuse to be downhearted, and here's the reason why:

I have a God who's mighty – who's sovereign and supreme;

I have a God who loves me, and I am on His team.

He is all-wise and powerful - Jehovah is His name;

Though everything is changeable, My God remains the same

My God knows all that's happening - Beginning to the end;

His presence is my comfort; He is my dearest Friend.

When sickness comes to weaken me - to bring my head down low,

I call upon my mighty God; into His arms I go.

When circumstances threaten rob me of my peace,

He draws me close unto His breast where all my strivings cease.

When my heart melts within me, and weakness takes control,

He gathers me into His arms - He soothes my heart and soul.

The great "I AM" is with me - my life is in His hand;

The "God of Jacob" is my hope; it's in His strength I stand.

I refuse to be defeated - My eyes are on my God;

He has promised to be with me as through this life I trod.

I'm looking past all my circumstances to Heaven's throne above.

My prayers have reached the heart of God – I'm resting in His love.

I give God thanks in everything - My eyes are on His face.

The battle's His, the victory mine; He'll help me win the race.

Don't Quit!

Author unknown

When things go wrong, as they sometimes will,

When the road you're trudging seems all uphill,

When the funds are low and the debts are high,

And you want to smile, but you have to sigh,

When care is pressing you down a bit-

Rest if you must, but don't you quit!

Life is queer with its twists and turns,

As every one of us sometimes learn,

And many a fellow turns about,

When he might have won had he stuck it out.

Don't give up though the pace seems slow,

You may succeed with another blow,

Often the goal is nearer than

It seems to a faint and faltering man.

Often the struggler has given up.

When he might have captured the victor's cup,

And he learned too late when night came down,

How close he was to the golden crown.

Success is failure turned inside out-

The silver tint of the clouds of doubt.

And you never can tell how close you are.

It may be near when it seems afar:

91

So stick to the fight when you're hardest hit-
It's when things seem worst you mustn't quit.

THE LITTLE RED WAGON

By Kimberlee Ann Burlik

During her tenth summer

She loved playing mommy to baby sister

Each day baby climbed into the little red wagon

Pleading for a ride.

Because she loved the cargo

Little mommy pulled the wagon.

Looking ahead, she pulled with strong fervor.

After all, baby needed mommy!

Over the summer, it became routine.

Little mommy had found her call.

Summer passed

As did the years.

Because she loved pulling the wagon,

Little mommy pulled the cargo.

Looking ahead, she pulled with tired determination.

After all, this was her duty!

But it became a drudgery

And little mommy was exhausted.

Glancing behind, she groaned,

"How did you all get in my wagon?

I can't keep pulling much longer."

(Baby sister had been joined by daddy

And friends and even some strangers!)

Looking bewildered. They all screamed,

"Stop your pulling and we'll get out!"

Chapter 19

Fiery Darts

"Be self-controlled and alert.
Your enemy, the devil prowls around
Like a roaring lion looking
For someone to devour.
Resist him,
Standing firm in the faith,
Because you know that your brothers
Throughout the world
Are undergoing the same
Kind of sufferings."
I Peter 5:8,9

J anuary, February, March, three months of the year that seems to drag the home schooling Mom into the deepest despair. Many cling to the term "burnout!" They feel their involvement with the children all day is too much. Then there are church activities, sports activities and struggling to know if the curriculum is too loose or too strict has finally come to a peak and they cannot take it anymore! This is the time when many home schooling mothers feel like putting the children in school. We feel like maybe that's the answer to all the turmoil! We might even begin to dream of that spotless house or just having free time to go get a haircut, do a craft project, or take a soak.

After experiencing this a couple of times (nearly every year) and discussing it with other mothers who have also gone through the same thing, I am convinced it is a combination of events prior to and during these three months which really affect the home schooling mother. It is during these times that I believe Satan seizes the opportunity to capitalize upon our feelings of inadequacy, thus rendering us ineffective.

The Struggles

Let's take a look at what happens during these months. First of all, we are returning from the excitement of Thanksgiving/Christmas holidays (created by the world and it's materialism) and we find that getting back into the routine of school in January is difficult.

Depending on the area of the country you live in, you could be facing cold, bleak winter days. Children can't get out to play and if they do, there's a grand ordeal to go through with getting them dressed and undressed into snowsuits or coats, gloves, and hats. Then there's the clean up after they come back into the house… The weather can and does often affect one's outlook on life. This is also the flu season. Illnesses and colds can lock up a Mom in the home for weeks at a time. Also, Uncle Sam is beginning to bless all of our homes with income tax booklets and statements are coming in the mail. If someone hasn't been carefully keeping records, this could be a tense and trying time. Before you know it, you're into February and much of the same difficulties can be found. Most couples halfheartedly celebrate the month at a couples' dinner but never really get to spend true time together. Tension mounts, tempers flare; quiet times are few and far between. You're not as organized with the school records or papers as you'd like to be. Doubts have been flooding in and you may have even called a local Christian school. You don't really plan to do it, but just knowing it's a possible option seems to sooth you for the moment. You wonder if you're doing the right thing…

Then, comes the month of March. The fear of testing is just around the corner. You wonder if you've done enough or taught the right things. You feel like it's not a test of your child's skill, but a test of your teaching ability. You start to pull away from activities that are not absolutely necessary, because you want to get down to academics. Before you know it, you feel isolated from other women and you think you're the only one going through this.

The Fiery Darts

In his usual cunning way, Satan has found a fault in your armor. Let me remind you of some facts. God has placed these children in our families and homes for a short time to be nurtured, cared for, loved, trained, and presented with the gospel. Satan would love nothing more than to have you defeated. He will attack at every opportunity he is given. He loves to steal, kill and destroy. For home schoolers, he will attack in the area of our relationships— with our husbands and our children. What can you do?

The Answer

First, humble yourself before the Lord. Give your burdens over to Him. Remember Galatians 2:20. Relieve yourself of the burden of feeling like you (as Mom) or you (as parents) are the sole individuals responsible for the education of your child. God gave this child two parents and He placed them in a world that He created. He has already made provision for them. Daily, go before the Lord and ask for wisdom in educating your child/children. Find and claim several Scripture verses. Abide in His presence and in prayer. While you are a vital part of your child's education, you are one of many individuals whom God will use to grow this child to maturity. I define education as the journey of life. I believe it is a private, intimate, personal relationship between a student and his teacher. For the Christian, God our heavenly Father is the ultimate source of authority. Through the teachings and life examples of His son, Jesus Christ, and the divine guidance of the Holy Spirit, education is the journey of life toward growth and maturity in Christ. The definition of teacher cannot be confined to simply one or two human individuals. Learning can take place anytime and anywhere! We as parents are the "earthen vessels" through whom God works. As we daily seek God's will in the education of HIS children, he will make the path of education straight! It will not be completed at the end of grade twelve.

The Pressure

(Fear, Guilt, Comparison)

Many of us are causing our children and ourselves undue stress and pressure. We tend to constantly compare our children with children in the public or Christian schools. We don't mean to, but inwardly, we may be looking at other children we know when we want our children to read, write, or do better in math. One year I was especially concerned about my children's penmanship and language arts skills. I tried every creative way I could think of to get them to write. It was like pulling teeth! I had the opportunity to speak with a Christian who taught in a local public school struggling with the same problem in her class. This teacher told me of the new Language Arts Program in her school. She was not allowed to use her traditional readers, spellers, or phonics books. The children would be allowed to write, write, write, even if the spelling words were incorrect. They were also encouraged to read, read, read, beginning with the simple words and building up. "They're trying to get authors this year," she said rather matter-of-factly. That bothered me. It was a grim reminder of my own last years in high school when at that time they needed people with business degrees in the work force. As a result, I took courses I wasn't even interested in and eventually dropped out of college. No child can be expected to write without a proper introduction to the formation of letters and to read without the proper introduction to phonics (correct pronunciation of the sounds of the letters). This foundation is the foundation a child will draw from for the rest of his or her life. I later discovered that the problem was not with our children, it was with my methods of teaching and the curriculum that I was using.

God's Way

God has a plan for my children. He may want them to become carpenters, missionaries, computer specialists, pastors, teachers, mechanics, doctors, fathers & mothers, lawyers, etc. I should not pattern my children after the world. As Romans 12:2 states "do not conform any longer to the pattern of this world, but be transformed by the renewing of your mind. Then you will be able to test and approve what God's will is - His good, pleasing and perfect will."

The Benefits of Home Schooling

Another teacher friend of mine bragged on having 20 to 30 minutes of class time to read. That sounded good at first, until one realizes that in a classroom full of thirty children, there is no way a teacher can monitor their progress or correct their enunciation of words. How will she know if all thirty truly comprehend the material until she gives a test? If it is multiple choice, they could guess, so that would not be a true assessment of their ability. We home schoolers are so blessed! We are able to stay home and educate our children. We can meet the individual needs of our children right on the spot. We can sit and read together, moving from the recognition of the sound each letter makes to decode the word. We can use fingers to point at words, or bookmarks to hold under a sentence. We can know exactly where our child is functioning! We can read in the morning, afternoon, or at night. We can read while waiting in the car, the dentist, or doctor's office. We can have the children read to us while we work. We can spend 30 minutes, or an hour or more, if we so choose. We are blessed that we can give the individual attention needed right when they need it.

People often ask, "How are you going to teach the hard subjects like Biology, Chemistry or Algebra?" I was faced with this dilemma of teaching a subject I had no knowledge in when our eight-year-old son Michael decided he wanted to build a motor and study electricity. I thought to myself, *I don't know anything about motors or electricity*! But we went to the library and I let him loose (under my supervision of course) in the section of books he desired. He discovered how to use the screen to find the locations of the books. He discovered the numbering system of the Library (Math) and other literary works both bad and good (Discernment). The door was opened to independent learning. I marveled at his ability to build not only a motor from scratch materials, but also a light bulb and simple radio. Once the basics of reading and simple math facts were achieved, he was able to build from there.

We did not throw out all the workbooks nor some of our curriculum choices. There were times when our children needed the repetition of a workbook for penmanship, grammar or math facts. How else would they learn to form correct letters or remember numbers unless there is some consistency in the model they follow? At that point, some of our other children had not reached the stage of independent learning. They needed lots of one-on-one time especially in the area of reading and math. They were struggling learners. This was especially demanding on me during the day as I went from child to child, trying to help them understand. I later learned to share the load with Dad at night. Once the children discovered an interest in a subject, we found this to be very motivating. Their desire to know more created a strong urge for learning. They wanted to learn how to read so that they could do it for themselves. This independent learning gave them a sense of accomplishment.

Get Help

(A Friend, Book, Teacher, Seminar, Professional)

Second, seek the help when you need it. The answer might be found in a book, a seminar, a neighbor, an acquaintance, a friend, a teacher, or a professional. As brothers and sisters in Christ, we need each other! We are interdependent. Learn how to network with others, especially those who have already gone through it. Seek those who are older, wiser or more experienced. Some of us act like we're floating through unchartered waters. We act as if no other parent in the world has ever experienced this before. At this time, there have been enough books written and enough human beings around to aid you in whatever you're going through. Several years ago, a friend expecting her 6th and 7th (twins) was concerned about how she was going to home school. She was advised by Dorothy Moore to put those babies on a schedule instead of demand feeding. "That," she said, "would bring more order," to my friend's life. While many of us might cringe at the thought of neglecting that poor baby if it cried even once, we are forgetting about the sin nature that is very present in that little one. If we are not careful, we will be obeying it instead of being the ones in authority.

Third, we need the love and support of our husbands. After we have dealt with interruptions, uncooperative children at times, unfinished school work, unfinished housework, unfinished projects, etc. etc. etc., it begins to wear a mother down. We may begin to feel worn-out and burned out! Let's face it, home schooling is not only mentally demanding, but it is spiritually, emotionally, and physically exhausting. Depending on the job, our husbands may enjoy the benefit of completing a project and receiving a sense of accomplishment of a task. As mothers in the home, we do not receive that same type of reward. There is always another dish to wash, book to read, assignment to complete, and an errand to run. While our husbands may have the benefit of promotions, bonuses, or feed back from peers or the boss, we in the home are limited to our husbands, our children, friends at church, and potential critical family member or neighbor. I do believe we get feedback, but it takes a lot longer. For example, after working with a child for over a year or more to accomplish the task of reading, he or she may suddenly start picking up words and reading. Oh, the joy! Oh, the reward! Or after teaching manners, behaviors, or job skills, we may see progress. But we don't often see it on a day-to-day basis. When my husband compliments something that has taken place in our home schooling experience when he returns from work, those little words of affirmation mean so much to me!

But what really helps most is when he takes an active part in home schooling. Sometimes he needs to come in and be the principal. When I have not been firm and consistent, he needs to step in (in love and firmness, not anger) and take charge. At other times, I just need him to listen and give me his objective opinion or feedback.

Then there are the times when I need him to vacuum, wash clothes or dishes, teach a subject, read a book to the children, drill them in spelling, phonics, or math. Sometimes, I'll need him to ask questions from the Bible lesson, history lesson or about the field trip. Sometimes, I need him to be a mind reader. You know what I mean? See the need then meet it. For example, there was a time (more times than I care to admit) when the home schooling clutter covered my entire kitchen counter. It didn't matter that I cleaned it off each day or several times a day-it always seemed to be piled up at the end of the day. I simply didn't have a specific place for the books and the other things to be. I asked my husband to build me a cabinet where books and most of our supplies could be kept. Somehow, I felt this would be the answer that would help organize our home and school activities. Months later, he surprised me with a newly built cabinet. We had a place to keep all of our books and supplies. He came home to a clean counter and a cheerful wife!

Practical Things You Can Do

- -Stay in God's Word. Abide in His presence.
- -Keep your priorities straight: God, Husband, Children, Others.
- -Limit your activities. Set aside special family time and especially couple time.
- -Educate yourself. Subscribe to a home schooling magazine or newsletter to minister to your specific needs. Read as many books or magazines as you can on home schooling.
- -Attend at least one seminar a year.
- -Participate in a support group.

---

*Draw a time line. Mark it in increments of 10 from 0 to 100. Give yourself plenty of space. This diagram will represent your years here on earth, assuming you will live to be that ripe old age. Mark the spot where you were married, where each child was born, and where they will be by age eighteen, nineteen or twenty. How much time will you have left in your adult years, assuming you will live that long? Now you can take this exercise further and reduce your years on earth, how much time will you have beyond those young parenting years? This little exercise always helps me to put into perspective just how short the time is that we have with our children. It also helps me to become even more determined to input as many good experiences as I can.

0-------10--------20---------30---------40---------50---------60---------70-------80---------90-------100

Let's Get Practical

Will you take a few minutes to answer the following questions?

Rate the following on a scale of 1 to 10

(#1 - Lowest/Unsuccessful, #10 - Highest/Successful)

☐Quiet times (personal study of God's Word)_____ ☐Prayer Life_____

☐Proper Rest_____ ☐Eating Habits_____

☐Marriage Relationship_____ ☐Child/Parent

relationship_____

☐Family Times_____ ☐Finances_____

☐Sin in your life_____ (Scores of 5 or less reflect the need for change in that area)

Food For Thought

1.   Do you know the difference between "school at home" versus "home school"? _____

2.   Do you have a balance between Bible teaching/ chores/ schoolwork/ fields trips/ free time for creative expression? _____

3.   Have you and your husband arrived at a mutual philosophy for education? _____

4.   Have you and your husband set individual goals for each child? _____

5.   Do you have an orderly home? _____

6.   Do you rise in the morning, before, with, or after your children? _____

7.   Do you have a plan for the day the night before? _____

8.   Do you and your husband have an agreed upon method of child discipline? _____

9.   Do you believe there is more than one way to accomplish a goal? _____

10.   Do you view yourself as a professional? _____

11.   Do you view yourself as an ambassador for Jesus Christ? _____

12.   Do you receive any home schooling magazines? _____

    Which one? _____

13.   Do you read at least one book on home schooling per year? _____

14.   How long have you home schooled? _____

15.   When was the last time you did something for yourself?

_____

What did you do? _____

16.   Why do you think home schooling is no longer fun? _____

_____

_____

_____

17.   What expectations do you have for your child/children?

_____

_____

_____

_____

18.   Does your child's performance match your expectations?_____

_____

_____

19.   Is the material you are using, age appropriate or student appropriate? _____

20.   Do you know your child's learning style? _____ Yours? _____

21.   Have you considered the option to seek professional medical or educational help?

_____

22.   Have you fasted and prayed? _____

Remember everyone wants:

- Love
- Acceptance
- Security
- Significance
- Direction

When the weather gets cold the Cross men go sledding ...

Continue On

By Roy Lessin

A woman once fretted over the usefulness of her life. She feared she was wasting her potential being a devoted wife and mother. She wondered if the time and energy she invested in her Husband and children would make a difference. At times she got discouraged because so much of what she did seemed to go unnoticed and unappreciated. "Is it worth it?" she often wondered. "Is there something better I could be doing with my time?" It was during one of these moments of questioning that she heard the still small voice of her heavenly Father speak to her heart. "You are a wife and mother because that is what I have called you to be. Much of what you do is hidden from the public eye. But I notice. Most of what you give is done without remuneration. But I am your reward. Your husband cannot be the man I have called him to be without your support. Your influence upon him is greater than you think and more powerful than you will ever know. I bless him through your service and honor him through your love. Your children are precious to Me. Even more precious than they are to you. I have entrusted them to your care to raise for Me. What you invest in them is an offering to Me. You may never be in the public spotlight. But your obedience shines as a bright light before Me. Continue on. Remember you are my servant. Do all to please Me."

Chapter 20

The Fear of Testing

"The fear of the Lord is the beginning of knowledge."
Proverbs 1:7

'Do not conform any longer to the pattern of this world, but be transformed by the renewing of your mind.
Then you will be able to test and approve what God's will is - His good, pleasing and perfect will."
Romans 12:2

"Search me, O God, and know my heart; Test me and know my anxious thoughts."
Psalm 139; 23

I 'll never forget the day I handed one of our children a test to take. I had everything ready-from the number two pencils and the test booklet, to the quiet atmosphere. After getting my child settled in a private room of our home, I left for a few minutes. When I returned, I found the answer sheet totally destroyed with black splotches and long scratches that whirled up, down and all around the paper.

I was furious. I was totally embarrassed. I was befuddled. *Why did our child do this*? I wondered. He was eight years old and surely able to begin testing. I grimaced as I had to make the call to the teacher at the testing center in another state. At that time we belonged to the Hewitt Research Foundation started by Dr. Moore. I felt humiliated that our child had ruined this testing sheet. When I explained what had happened to the teacher, it didn't seem to concern or bother her one bit. "He's not ready." she said matter-of-factly, "Try again next year."

She was right, by the next year this child had improved in his ability to read and write. This child had gained confidence in his ability to bubble in the answers. I spent much more time preparing all of the children for the test taking experience. I began keeping notes, on the back of each test result with my observations and stating the facts of exactly what was going on in the life of the child during that test taking period.

There were years when I disagreed even giving the children tests. Since we worked so closely together, I was able to look at a test and know immediately how well or how poorly the children would perform. I knew this because I knew what subjects we covered and to what extent we delved into the material. I also knew the level of difficulty the children were working. At that time, I knew very little about the portfolio approach and was unsure about how to do it. Michael insisted that we take standardized achievement test each year. I followed his advice, and years later I was very glad that I had these records. In the specific case of the one child experiencing difficulty in learning, it was very helpful to have documentation and proof of the progress this child made while home schooling when I needed to seek professional help.

Many years later, we were participating in group testing with our support group. The halls were buzzing with children and mothers-each trying to find their way to the correct room. There was both an air of excitement and anxiety. I passed several mothers with toddlers in tow and babies on hips as I rushed to drop seven-year-old Matthew off in the Kindergarten room. I overheard two mothers sharing about their fear and panic at having to test. "Well," said one mother, "now comes the test of my teaching ability. We'll see if I taught them anything."

Our support group had several mothers with degrees who were volunteering to be the test administrators. Those without degrees volunteered for other jobs such as nursery duty, playground duty, or hall monitor. Since most of the mothers' did not know what to do with these test results after they came back, another mother who was certified to teach and I drafted an article concerning the myths of testing.

We noticed incorrect thinking amongst home schoolers so we first answered the question, "Why do we test?" We determined that the real purpose of testing was basically to assess yearly progress of a student and to respond to the requirement of our state laws. There were other myths, like the myth that testing was a measure of a parents' ability to teach, or that testing measures all the student has possibly learned for that school year.

Variables

In our search and from our previous testing experiences, we found many variables that can affect the outcome of a test session:

1. The test administrator had not given proper instructions.

2. The test administrator was not properly prepared in test taking procedures such as bubbling, timed section, unsharpened #2 pencils, etc.

3. The parents' selection of the wrong grade level for a child's' test.

4. The child had not received adequate rest.

5. The child had health problems.

6. The child was hungry and unable to concentrate.

7. The child was easily distracted by noise or was uncomfortable with a particular design of the furniture.

8. The child was distracted by the room temperature- either too hot or too cold.

9. The child was distracted by the table arrangement or the arrangement of certain students together.

10. The child's state of mind (fearful, overly excited, anxiety-parental pressure)

11. The child was distracted by life's circumstance such as a death in the family, job loss of a parent, a recent move, etc.

Testing Results

1. Test results without an explanations of terms or way of evaluating what the scores mean, the test results are useless.

2. Achievement testing is one indicator of assessing student performance.

3. Achievement tests do not measure your child's intellectual abilities.

What can you, the parent, do with these results?

1. Remember why you are home educating; go back to your family philosophy.

2. Keep accurate records of your child's learning progress.

3. Document your parental observations (i.e. child is not reading, ill, test anxiety, etc.)

Types of Tests*

Intelligence Tests

Tests, such as the <u>Stanford-Binet Intelligence Scale</u> and the <u>Wechsler Intelligence Scale for Children-III (WISC-III)</u>, measure memory, general knowledge, ability to see similarities, patterns, missing pieces, and absurdities, among other skills. A verbal and nonverbal score combine to create a general intelligence quotient (IQ) score.

Achievement Tests

<u>Wechsler Individual Achievement Test (WIAT)</u>- measures levels of reading, sight-word recognition, spelling, math computation, listening, and reading comprehension.

<u>Key Math Test</u>- measures basic concepts in math—such as time, measurement, estimation, sequencing, money, computation, and problem solving.

<u>Woodcock Johnson Psycho educational Battery</u>- measures cognitive abilities-such as memory and processing information, levels of achievement in math, reading, written language, and general knowledge.

Visual-Motor Tests

<u>Beery Visual-Motor Integration (VMI)</u> Test-measures ability to copy figures

Language Tests

<u>Peabody Picture Vocabulary Test</u>- measures receptive language ability

<u>Slingerland Screening Tests</u>-measures visual-motor skills, memory, visual, and auditory discrimination with regard to language skills.

<u>Test of Auditory Perceptual Skills (TAPS)</u>-measures auditory-processing skills, auditory memory, and ability to follow directions.

<u>Test of Language Development</u>-measures vocabulary, grammar, sentence construction, and word relationships.

Conclusion

1. It is unrealistic to expect that a single test wield so much weight.

2. There may be some discrepancy between test scores when using the unit study approach as opposed to traditional curriculum due to the content of the material being taught.

3. The possibility of error exists in marking the correct answer on the answer sheet.

3. The possibility of error exists in computer read scores.

4. OBE has crept into testing such as situational ethnics, attitudes, and feelings. In addition, early standards in testing have been lowered in order to reflect higher scores nationally.

Testing is in no way a measure of a parents' ability to teach! Testing cannot possibly measure all aspects of what a child has learned. There are simply too many variables that can alter results. Other issues may also be involved.

Chapter 21

The Friendship Connection - Support Groups

"A friend loveth at all times."
Proverbs 17:17
"There is a friend who sticks closer than a brother."
Proverbs 18:24
"Greater love has no one than this, that he lay down his life for his friends. You are my friends if you do what I command."
John 15:13

I t was the second Tuesday of the month, time for our monthly support group meeting. I had been asked to lead a small discussion group of newer home schooling moms. I glanced over at the clock, 6:15 p.m. "AHHH!! I'm going to be late," I huffed. I was about to head out of the door when an unusual sound caught my ear. "Gurgle, gurgle, gurgle, splash!" *What in the world is that,* I thought. I followed the sound to the downstairs bathroom and opened the door just in time to see the water overflowing from the toilet. "Oh no! I don't have time for this now!" I mouthed out as I called for the children to scramble and look for the Sears Power Vac. Now the water was headed down the hallway, into the kitchen and toward the living room carpet. *Maybe I shouldn't go tonight,* I thought. *Maybe this is a trick of the devil to get me distracted so I won't go and be encouraged by other moms.*

I shut the valve off behind the toilet bowl, and mopped up as much water as I could. One of the children had returned with the Shop Vac and was beginning to vacuum the rest of it off the floor. The other children were trying to dry the floor with old towels.

This was not the kind of end to an already difficult day with unruly, difficult little ones. I thought of the other mothers coming to the meeting and wondered what their days might have been like. *How can I encourage them Lord?* I wondered. Then I suddenly realized that they probably needed a friend, just like I did, someone who could understand and relate to what they were going through.

Even after I washed my hands several times, they still felt gross and dirty. I picked up a little bottle of nice smelling lotion and rubbed it onto my hands. The Lord gave me an idea.

At the meeting, Rhonda greeted me and told me how peaceful and together I always looked. She even told me that she wanted to be like me when she grew up. I smiled, *if only she knew*. I was so bummed out over my difficult day; it took all of the energy I had to walk into the church building for that meeting.

Later after the main meeting, we broke off into our small groups; I began the session by asking the ladies to share a little about their home school day. I handed each woman a small bit of lotion to rub into their hands as they spoke. While Rhonda's hands twisted back and forth slowing massaging the lotion in, she began to share about her family and recent struggles as a new home schooler. "I need to be more organized," she said. When I squirted the lotion into Cheryl's hand, she began to massage her hands and say, "you know, this is the first thing I've done for myself all day!" Others shared also, and I received such joy from God as He confirmed in my heart that He had given me the idea and a way to help each of us relax and share. We needed support. We needed encouragement. We needed friendship.

Truly, our family learned one of the best parts of home schooling was not only meeting new friends but also establishing friendships that helped each of us to carry the load of home schooling. We found it quite easy to begin a support group. We simply found a family or two who shared similar interests and it didn't take long for word of mouth to spread the news of a support group.

We found support groups to be very beneficial in attracting families like ourselves who were trying to accomplish similar goals. We found fathers and mothers with varied educational backgrounds and from a wide variety of professions. We found friends.

As we grew in our friendships within a support group, we were able to utilize the large number for group discounts at field trips, for book purchases or food co-ops. We were able to host book sales or curriculum fairs to benefit the group and the community. We were able to network for information. We were able to host science fairs, spelling bees, geography bees, testing, and a wide variety of classes such as art, drama, history, science, music, etc. We were able to visit the nursing homes. We were able to arrange for family or yearly home school portraits. We were able to invite speakers or one of the parents knowledgeable in a specific subject matter to address the group. We were able to host retreats for moms to get away. We were able to help each other in times of trouble. We were able to begin co-ops, where several families swapped teaching amongst the children.

The friendships our family and our children developed during these years were priceless. In fact, we believe God provided them along the way. We do offer a word of caution on support groups or co-ops: we must be careful and selective in the establishment of such bonds for many reasons. The Word of God gives us this reason: "He who walks with the wise grows wise, but a companion of fools suffers harm." Proverbs 13: 20

Below are a few of the friends we met and some of the things we learned:

Ohio folks (2001-2002) Chad & Kristen Andrews, Tim & Dawn Arceneaux, David & Jennifer Damron, Brent & JoAnn Davis, Michael & Cay Freels, Phil & Pam Gross, Scott & Michelle Leta, Bruce & Debbie Maddox, Matt & Merrill Spring, Barak & Victoria Strickland, Peter & Stephanie Wiza (1998-2000) Rick & Diane Allnutt, Tom & Renee Border, Glen & Gayle Campbell, Ken & Margaret Colvin, Tom & Sue Cutting, Dan and Amy Everett, Dean & Keriann Harkness, Jim & Tina Hocker, Steve & Elise Hocking, Jeffrey & Shannon Sanner, Mark & Kandice Speed, Bill & Lisa Weidenhammer, Jim & Bonny Williams.

Parent's Educating At Christian Homes & Friends (1993- 1997) Josephine Alderson, Tom & Kim Baird, Beverly Baker, Brian & Laurie Blair, Craig & Jeri Carson, Steven & Rhonda Chambers, Robert & Nancy Cook, Paul & Diane Cope, Mike & Sherry Cwiakala, Grover & Margaret Degler, Mick & Barb Denen, Jon & Elaine Dobney, Dave & Doris Evans, Lanny & Annette Fideler, Mark & Laurie Flower, Kenneth & Nancy French, Gary & Kaye Geist, Wynn & Paula Gifford, Jeff & Lisa Halsey, Pastor Wayne & Donna Hart, Ed & LeAnn Hill, Jerry & Joyce Hill, Mark & Dawn Mathews, Nelson & Sharon McKeever, Leonard & Merry Moses, John & Tammy Norckauer, Greg & Rhonda Osman, Gary & Diane Phelps, David & Libby Pidgeon, Greg & Donna Potts, Pastor Rex & Becky Robinson, Paul & Michelle Roebuck, Denny & Jeannie Roeck, Pastor & Mrs. Charles Savage, James & Mary Sellers, Doug & Sandy Sjoquist, Kathy Steiner, Chip & Rene Sutton, Mike & Karen Tucker, David & Linda Ulmer, Scott & Debbie Wills, Fred & Gilda Winkler, Ron & Patty Wright, Fred & Carol Zehring.

Virginia folks (1988-1993) Vicki Balduck, Chuck & Ann Evans, Jeff & Sue Graf, Mitch & Terri Hailstone, Mark & Paula Inglis, Ken & Mary Lewis, Frank & Betty Ann Lifsey, Woody & Claudia Long, Lee & Cherie Koss, Hugh & Bernie McGillicuddy, Tim & Linda McWilliams, John & Linda Medaris, Mark & Vicki Pier, Dave & Pat Pruden.

Virginia folks-continued (1988-1993) Pastor Andy & Diane Richardson, Jim & Lorena Rowe, Phil & Elena Schiener, Charles & Deborah Siler, Pastor Sam & Deanne Taylor, David & Sandy Wortley, Jonathan & Lisa Zellner, Jim & Lorie Zellner.

Nevada folks (1986 -1988) Keith & Waynette Young, and the one hundred families of Home Schools United-Vegas Valley.

We learned about orienteering, taking nature walks, art, drama, science, herbs, eating healthy foods, how to start a food co-op, quilting, knitting, crocheting, sign language, the art of giving, sharing, loving, geography, setting up field trips, editing a paper, book, making a place mat, making a basket, making a banner, marching in a parade, library skills, visiting the elderly, riding horses, sheep, goats, chickens, building barns, building houses. The list is endless…

Friends

By Amanda Bradley

*Friends will always
See you through,
Believe in things
You want to do,
Feel happy when
Your dreams come true-
That's just that way friends are.
Friends will always be right there
With wisdom, faith,
And strength to share,
With love that shows
How much they care-
That's just the way
Friends are.*

Enjoying our time at the Girls' Club meeting

Taking a walk with the Thompson's at Glen Helen Park in Ohio

A hayride with our friends at GRACE Home School Support Group in Virginia

Jacqueline Anne, Joyce, Bea, Sherman Davis from Accotink Academy in Virginia

Chapter 22

Better Homes and Gardens

"In my Father's house are many rooms; if it were not so, I would have told you.
I am going there to prepare a place for you. I will come back and take you to be with me
That you also may be where I am. You also may know the way to the place where I am going." John 14:2-4
"Unless the Lord builds the house, its builders labor in vain."
Psalm 127:1

"A wise woman builds her house,
But with her own hands the foolish one tears hers down."
Proverbs14:1

"The Lord's curse is on the house of the wicked,
But He blesses the home of the righteous."
Proverbs 3:33

We could barely open the door to enter my friends' house because the piles of clothing barred the way into the downstairs basement area. As my friend walked me through, she showed me all the work the family had been doing to build a playroom, extra bedrooms and a separate laundry area. With each room we passed, clutter was the theme. Toys, papers, projects and clothes were everywhere! My friend was embarrassed, but not embarrassed enough to stop or not show me around her home. She kept leading the way from room to room. When we arrived at the second level, the clutter theme repeated itself, right into the kitchen. Dishes were all over the table, across the counter and piles were in the sink. She showed me the rest of the house and all of the creative touches her husband had done to make the curtain rods and the children's beds. When she finished the tour, she invited the children and I to stay for dinner. Her husband was out of town and it was going to be a lonely week for her. She grimaced as she pulled the roast from the freezer, wondering what and how she was going to prepare it for a quick meal. While the children busied themselves with games inside and out, we set about clearing and cleaning in the kitchen. She didn't mind my help, so together while we talked, we washed the dishes, cleared the table and prepared the meal. We sat down to tea and chatted while the meat thawed and the potatoes boiled in the pot. Fresh veggies from the garden sat in the windowsill, so it was one less decision to make about the meal. We enjoyed our time together and within a few hours, we were enjoying a very tasty meal. We were treated to after dinner music by my musical son Michael and the other children who were aspiring to be pianists. We sang songs together and laughed at ourselves when it became obvious that several in the group could not carry a tune. Since night was beginning to fall, the children and I hurried home.

That visit has been etched in my memory for years. It will stand as a monument of a warm, loving, gracious, hospitable visit, though a chaotic one. Why? Because my hostess heart was focused on Christ, even though her house was in complete disarray. Through the hours of our conversation, her goal was obvious, though it did not show at that exact moment in time. The goal was godly offspring, a good marriage, fellowship with believers and a place to worship freely.

Prior to this time, our family had been blessed with opportunities to visit in many homes. We have been in homes where the tension was so tight that if a crumb dropped on the floor or a water ring were left by a glass of water, the hostess became frenzied and nervous. As guests in these types of homes, our only desire was to depart as quickly as possible.

For as many of my home schooling years as I can remember, I always desired for our home to be an orderly home. I loved the idea on the front cover of the Teaching Home Magazine where each family appears to have it all together. You know what I mean? The family on the cover of magazines with the matching dresses, vests, ties and of course in the background is a tidy house with all the books stacked neatly on the shelf or where the books are in front of the children who are studiously working from them. I desired the home where all the children wake up with smiles on their faces ready to begin their day in joy, zealous about accomplishing their tasks for the day. There always seemed to be someone out of sorts, someone needing correction or "spurring on toward love and good deeds." But no matter how hard I tried; maintaining an uncluttered home was always a struggle. There were always dishes to be done, laundry to be folded, schoolbooks sprawled across the kitchen counter or table. The only time we achieved "the look" was when the children went to bed and I cleaned the way I wanted or we as a family cleaned together. Our home always had the "lived in" look. **Always**!!

A Christ-Centered Home

Here are some of the lessons our family has learned:

- A home centered on Christ begins when two people who each have a personal relationship with Jesus Christ seek to please Him. Each must love the Lord their God with all of their hearts and all of their souls and all of their minds! Each spouse must be dedicated to the task of serving the Lord by obedience to His Word. Wives are to submit unto their husbands as unto the Lord. (Col. 3:18) Husbands are to love their wives as Christ loved the church and gave Himself as a ransom. (Col. 3:19) Children are to honor and obey their parents. (Col. 3:20)

- A home centered on Christ knows the goal: The kingdom of Heaven. When Jesus Christ left this earth, He left us with a command to go into all the world and preach the gospel. The Good News of freedom. His death upon the cross has opened the way for the forgiveness of sins and fellowship with God. His ascension back into heaven after his resurrection provided a way for us to receive the Holy Spirit. The Spirit of the Living God seals us who know Christ as personal Lord and Savior. The Spirit of God lives in us. He guides us, teaches us, comforts us and intercedes for us. As a kingdom of priests in the priesthood of believers, we are to spread the message that the King is alive and well and He is coming again to claim His own!

- A Christ-centered home realizes that each person is a gift from God. Each family member is part of a unit with lifelong ties. Each family is uniquely designed to make up a personal cheering section from birth until death. Family will be there to welcome a baby into the world. Family will remember to be the birthdays. Family will support through church activities, ballet, soccer, swimming, art, football, piano, scout programs, and a host of other things. Family will rally together for the special events and for the graduations. Family will celebrate at marriage vows, join in joys, travel through trials and mourn at death.

- The focus of our week should be Christ. We should center every moment and everyday in every way on Christ. We should prepare our hearts and minds daily by the study of His word. We should be preparing our godly offspring when we disciple and train them. We should be helping them to develop godly character of compassion, contentment, courage, decisiveness, dependability, determination, diligence, discernment, discretion, empathy, enthusiasm, faithfulness, generosity, gentleness, kindness, honesty, humility, initiative, integrity, joyfulness, loyalty, obedience, patience, purity, responsibility, reverence, self-control, tender-hearted, and thankfulness. Our bodies are His Holy Temple. Our bodies are His dwelling place. We must consider what we feed our minds and our bodies.

- We are a family both literally and spiritually! We are His body, the Body of Christ! Everybody must work together. Everybody must work and everybody must help. These jobs/chores in the home give each member in the family a sense of responsibility, purpose and accomplishment. These jobs in the home prepare us for jobs outside of the home either in the local church or in the world to provide for ourselves, for family and for others.

- Father should take the lead in reading the Word to his family. This provides an opportunity for the wife and children to visibly see him in the spiritual role of leader that God has been given to him.

- We must learn to treat others the way we want to be treated.

- We must learn to forgive-give up our rights to be angry! Jesus gives us a "Free Pass" from "the Past."

- We must learn not to harbor bitterness or anger. We must learn to release it and let it go, for His mercies are new every morning!

- We must love one another! We must love with compassion and understanding. We must seek to be reconciled to one another.

- We must pray! Prayer is communication with God. We are not talking to a black hole in the sky, but we are speaking to a person, the one and only true God in three persons (Father, Son and Holy Spirit). We are in a love relationship with Him. This communication goes two ways, therefore we may speak but we must also listen, learn from Him, and respond to Him.

- We must learn to be content no matter what the circumstances. We must accept our station in life. Whether you are a carpenter, police officer, plumber, lawyer, banker, military officer, professor, mechanic, pastor, teacher, etc. etc.

- We must work and work hard! Idle hands and minds are the devil's workshop! Michael and I had two different philosophies about work. He liked to do what I considered "bulldoze through the work," meaning you work until it's finished and who cares if anyone is happy about it, there's work to be done. I liked to have fun while we worked! I wanted to enjoy the whole process as we worked, to take the focus off of it being so hard or monotonous. I desired for us as a family to derive the pleasure of working as unto the Lord and find joy in doing that. The children learned two sides of work.

- We must teach proper manners such as social graces, telephone and table manners. If you don't, who will? When the children were younger, I placed a large sign by our telephone. It read, "Hello, Cross residence, may I help you?" This made it easier for them not to have to guess at what to say. We invited other families over for meals. The children learned to set the table, decorate, make place cards out of index cards, and to be a host or hostess.

- We must plant no weed seeds! There should be no negative, critical words or remarks. There should not be yelling, screaming, yanking, jerking, name-calling, evil thoughts or suspicions and if you do, remember, "Love covers a multitude of sins." Michael and I came from different backgrounds, his Jamaican and mine American. Different parents raised us, his had three children, and mine had thirteen together. We each inherited a sinful nature. Therefore, in raising our children, we found it imperative to abide in God's Word that our words might be seasoned with His grace.

- We must not covet. The grass only looks greener on the other side. Through the years as we met and interacted with various families, it was obvious that we each home schooled from different socioeconomic levels. There were many times when as I entered friend's home, I would utter the words, "Thou shalt not covet thy neighbor's ox nor ass nor anything that is that neighbors." We must learn to be content with what we have.

- We must actively get involved in creating an atmosphere for an active, healthy, love life as a couple. We must continue to grow in our friendship with each other. We must read good books and go on dates to spend quality time together.

- We must love our spouses' body as if it were our own (because it is). Your spouse is God's gift to you.

- We must learn to incorporate lots of laughter, fun, and even play along with work at times.

- We must learn to "stand in the gap" for one another. Some home schooling mothers and fathers are coming from difficult and diverse backgrounds. We desire a better life for our children, but are hard pressed to pull from a foundation that is not there. For some, there is no pool of Christian virtues or biblical knowledge from which to draw. It is complete "O.J.T." called "on the job training." There are mothers and fathers who didn't have Christian mothers or fathers to teach them. Some are products of divorce. Some come from physically, sexually or emotionally abusive homes. Some come from sinful past in which a choice was made to abandon God's ways. A husband or a wife may be required to "stand in the gap" for a spouse who is for whatever reason unable to work up to their God-given position.

- We must pass on the baton of faith. The spiritual foundation we lay will affect the next generation. We must share the praiseworthy deeds of the Lord with our children.

- We must keep our faith an active living faith by responding to the call of God working amongst the people of this world.

- We must get involved when He invites us.

Myths About the Home

This is an area where we must be frank about the reality of home schooling. There are myths concerning home educating. <u>Don't fall for them</u>!

Myth #1 Your family should look like the family on the cover of the Teaching Home Magazine. Throughout our home schooling years, we have often compared ourselves to the front cover of the Teaching Home Magazine. Many, many, times we felt like we fell short of the lovely picture on the cover. Of course, we violated Scripture by comparing ourselves in the first place, but every family desires a model, a hero if you will. The Teaching Home Magazine does set a great standard for home schooling families. As a military family moving from country-to-country, state-to-state and house-to-house, we have had numerous opportunities to set up house. Our house has always had "the lived in look," because people lived there **FULL** time. A friend of mine gave me a sign that hangs near my front door. It says "If you've come to see me, Welcome! If you've come to see my house, make an appointment! In all of our striving to achieve this vision of what we thought our house should look like, we have come close, but never arrived at a perfectly well kept house. In our house, life often seems to be moving toward chaos. Someone has to be somewhere for something! Something is always breaking down! If it's not the heating element on the stove or dryer breaking, it's the icemaker on the refrigerator or the metal drawer hangers in the cabinets or the battery dying in the car or the lawn tractor. If it's not the laundry or the bills piling up, then it's the family organization or communication breaking down. In our house, training for life is occurring, therefore, chaos is inevitable. Life is always moving toward chaos, and it takes a tremendous amount of effort and energy to organize and work toward achieving anything!

Myth #2 My house should be perfectly clean with everything in order, including my husband, children and myself.

Everything will **<u>not</u>** be perfect and in order! There is much life being lived within each home. In homes with the lived in look, there may be times when: 1) Books, pamphlets, or bills may cover the kitchen counter, table, nightstand or bedroom floor. 2 The kitchen sink may not be empty or shiny because we had to make other things a priority. Things like giving birth, or taking care of a baby or sick child at night or behavioral correction (which will take quite a bit of time during the young years) or extending hospitality to a guest [a new home schooling family a college student, a family visiting the church, a stressed mother, a neighbor, etc. etc] 3) There may be times when toys, trash, stray wood from projects, string, tape or glue, animal shavings, grass, etc. etc may be displayed in various areas of the house. 4) There may be times when the children's academics are more important than cleaning up. 6) There may be times when going on a field trip takes precedence over cleaning up. 7) There may be times when cleaning up is more important than academics or field trips.

Myth #3 Your children need socialization with the outside world.

If you are truly home educating your children, you will have ample opportunities for socialization. As families participate in the day-to-day life experiences, they will live in the world and function in society. They will be socialized, sometimes more than you desire.

Myth #4 Your child will be brainy and go to Harvard.

Though all children should be aiming for the highest academic standards possible, not all home educated children will excel academically.

Myth #5 You fill in the blank_____

Realities About The Home

Reality #1 We must recognize the sovereignty of God and the freewill of man.

We must face the fact that God is the potter and we are the clay. He is our creator and can do with His earthen vessels what He wills. Ever since Adam and Eve, mankind has made both good and bad choices. We and our children have a freewill. We can and will continue to make both good and bad choices.

Reality #2 We (as Christians) are strangers and aliens here on this earth.

This place is not our home. We must "store our treasures in heaven where moths do not corrupt and thieves do not break in and steal." We are stewards of the things God has given us. We are caretakers of these children God has entrusted to our care. We must hold loosely those things that are not our possessions.

Reality #3 We are not perfect parents.

We will not do everything perfectly right in our home schools. We can aim for perfection but we will not achieve it. We will make many, many mistakes. We will do the best we can with the knowledge we have at the time.

Reality #4 We do not have perfect children.

Our children, no matter how hard we try or how many Bible lessons we teach, will make mistakes. They will, at some point in their lives make bad choices. If not, they would be perfect. The state of perfection exists only in glorified bodies when we reach our destination called heaven.

Reality #5 Home education is a way of life. It is a choice.

Because we as parents have chosen to educate in this particular manner, there are consequences to this choice. Home education is the experiential route of learning. It incorporates many different facets of teaching and of learning. It is demanding and requires total commitment on everyone's part.

Your family's socioeconomic level will affect your home schooling endeavors. The number of children you have will also affect your way of life. Your age and energy level may affect your home schooling activities. The bottom line is that home education is a way of life. Each family will learn to adapt to their specific situation and their specific needs.

Gardens

Human life began in the Garden of Eden, with God's creation of man. (Genesis 2:8) Man's first responsibility was to "work it and take care of it." (Genesis 2:15) Next, God formed a helper suitable for this man called her woman. (Genesis 2:23) Reflecting upon what God's word teaches concerning the woman He said "I will greatly increase your pains in childbearing; with pain you will give birth to children. Your desire will be for your husband, and he will rule over you." (Genesis 3:16) and to the man He said, "Cursed is the ground because of you; through painful toil you will eat of it, all the days of your life." (Genesis 3:17) Have either of these two statements made by the Lord God Himself changed for men and women today?

Today, God continues His work all around us! It is important for us to teach our children to work and to work hard. God had a purpose then and it has not changed. The purpose of a garden is for good healthy food, medicine for healing, and the serenity discovered in watching and enjoying Gods miracle of creation.

Let us also remember, the garden tomb. It was here that our Lord and Savior Jesus Christ was placed in a new tomb, in a garden. (John 19:41) As one poet wrote, "For Jesus found peace in a garden, when death marked the path He trod…" Recently, the Lord allowed me to discover a place in Covington, Kentucky called "The Garden of Hope." In 1938 a pastor Morris Coers visited the Holy Land and wished that all people could experience what he did there in the original garden tomb. In 1958, his dream became a reality when a replica of the tomb was dedicated here in the United States atop a hill in Covington. On September 29, 2000, on the eve of Rosh Hashanah, as one of the current gardener's Mr. Walter Preston, opened the tomb for my daughter Jennifer and I to enter, I wasn't sure how I felt about the experience. I anticipated something, but felt nothing. We stood there in the slightly darkened cold tomb for a while listening to the caretaker tell us about the place and a few of his experiences there for the last forty years. It wasn't until we excited the tomb that I suddenly became inspired. While the warm sun hit my face, I turned midway in the stony opening and said to the gardener, "the greatest part about this tomb is that it is empty and that gives us hope because He's alive!" Together, in that garden, we rejoiced.

In conclusion, a better home and garden is more clearly revealed in the loving relationships between family members. It is reflected as mothers and fathers interact with one another in a harmony produced through obedience to God's word and through His love.

It is reflected in the laughter and play of children. It is reflected in the agony of disappointments or the thrill of achievements. It is reflected in the support and encouragement given by one another. It is reflected in the discipline administered to a disobedient, wayward child. It is reflected in the joy of sharing life with family, friends and others. It is reflected in lives submitted to God's will.

Grandpops Owen & Grandmoms Audrey visit for Thanksgiving

Uncle & Aunt loving nephew Shaun   **Micah at work**

The Hearts' Garden

Author Unknown

The heart is like a garden

Where thought flowers grow

The thoughts that we think

Are the seeds that we sow

Every kind loving thought

Has a kind loving deed

While a thought that is selfish

Is just like a weed

We must watch what we think

Each minute all day

And put out the weed thoughts

And throw them away

And plant loving seed thoughts

So thick in a row

That there will not be room

For weed thoughts to grow.

The Invitation

By Danise Hahlbolm

You are invited to come dine with Me,

From now through all eternity,

Believe in the Father, Son & Holy Ghost,

And dine with Jesus as your host.

To live in Heaven eternally,

All you must do is

R.S.V.P.

"Do not forget to entertain strangers,
For by doing so some have entertained angels without knowing it."
Hebrews 13:2

"Likewise, teach the older women to be reverent in the way they live, not to be slanderers or
addicted to much wine, but to teach what is good. Then they can train the younger women to
love their husbands and children, to be self-controlled and pure, to be busy at home, to be
kind, and to be subject to their husbands, so that no one will malign the word of God."
Titus 2:3-5

Excuse This House

Author Unknown

Some houses try to hide the fact

That children shelter there

Ours boast of it quite openly

The signs are everywhere

For smears are on the windows

Little smudges in the doors

I should apologize I guess…

For toys strewn on the floor.

But I sat down with the children

And we played and laughed and read

And if the doorknob does not shine

Their eyes will shine instead

For when at times I am forced

The one job or the other

I want to be a housewife-

But first, I will be a mother.

Let's Get Practical

Definition of a mother: "Gentle among you, like a mother caring for her little children" II Thessalonians. 2:7

Definition of a father: "We dealt with each of you as a father deals with his own children, encouraging, comforting, and urging you to live lives worthy of God, who calls you into His Kingdom & glory." II Thessalonians. 2:11,12

A Christ-Centered Home

Begin each day acknowledging God's Sovereignty and Presence in your lives.

1. Each person should have individual devotions.

2. Pray as a couple (Father prays for mother, children & others; Mother prays for Father, children & others). These prayers will continue throughout the day as you each pray without ceasing, making all kinds of requests before God.

3. Family devotions (may be with Mom if Dad is off to work or may be in the evening)

4. Arm yourselves, put on the whole armor of God. (As home schoolers, the enemy does not want you to produce Godly offspring. The enemy will come against you in many ways! Remember Ephesians 6:1 and John 17: 26. You must fight and work hard at keeping the ways of the world out of your home and keeping the focus on family and doing God's will.

5. Aim activities for the week toward worship and fellowshipping with God, family, and other believers (i.e. pre-plan meals, clothing for Sunday, clean the home, create a quiet /loving atmosphere)

6. Low impact exercises/Healthy meals. You body is His temple, the dwelling place of the Holy Spirit. Keep it fit, healthy and disease free.

Character

Godly character is a Christian parents' goal for their children. We must model it before them and find many ways to creatively teach it throughout our time together. The Bible is our foundation for this, but through a combination of Bible teaching, good books, videos, relationships, and experiences, a child's character will be developed. We must purposely teach character.

Eliminate the F A T! Frustration, Anger & Tension

If you find your home filled with frustration, anger, and tension, these are clues that something is wrong. It may be in our expectations, it may be due to sin, or it may be due to miscommunication. These issues should be dealt with immediately and not allowed to go beyond the setting of the sun. Allowing them to pile up will only create more frustration, anger and tension. Sometimes this build up will cause an explosion of ungodly behavior. "Anger does not bring about the righteous life that God requires of you." Discipline is for the purpose of training in righteousness, not for the pain of punishment.

Chores

"We are a family, everybody helps." In order to function as a family unit in the home, things work best when family members are assigned areas of responsibility. There are many ways to accomplish this goal. The bottom line is that the jobs in the home should be identified and each family member should take responsibility in accomplishing various tasks. Parents should work together to determine what needs are essential and critical before assembling the family to discussion or assignments. Often times, this job of home management falls to the mother, but unity is better achieved if approached as a family.

1. Laundry - Put in a load first thing in the morning or a load on the night before. Either way, you can start a load of wash or throw clothes into the dryer then sit/kneel for your quiet time. The laundry is a critical part of functioning in the home. Many activities center on having clean clothes available for our ability to do the things we want outside of our homes. In simple terms, if there is not a clean item to wear or an item is not ironed and ready to wear, it does affect the stress level in the family. Keep the laundry baskets, in the laundry room. Folding laundry in other rooms of the house just creates clutter all over the house.

2. Mail - From the mailbox to a mail basket. Always open mail with the trashcan underneath. Deal with it the first time instead of reading it, then leaving it on the table for a second go round then a third time before actually dealing with it. Bills can be placed in a bill rack, magazines can go to a table, basket or magazine holder, and personal letters can receive an immediate response if you're prepared with stationery and stamps. Often times, I

will tear off the advertisement of a bill, remove statement portion from portion to be returned then stamp the return envelope. With the Internet no E-mail changing the way we do business and the way we communicate, it is still possible to coordinate and organize your mail. Remember the delete button!

3. Garbage - Garbage in, garbage out. Continual upkeep and maintenance are necessary.

4. Grocery List - Since most families rotate through the same menu approximately every two weeks, by organizing your meals, you can add different items and incorporate new ideas. You can easily set up a menu by asking each family member what his or her favorite breakfast, lunch and dinner meal is. Then, arrange alternate meals between those, Start with one week. Next, work into two, three or more meals per month at a time. Always work toward the best possible nutritious meal, living foods (fresh vegetables, fresh fruits, whole grains) as opposed to dead food (in a can, frozen, overly cooked). We Americans eat too much food. Our portions are too large and it shows. Obesity in America has reached a dangerous/deadly level. The supplementation of vitamins and minerals is no longer an option, but a necessity for proper nutrition. Also, since the human body is made of 80% water, drink at least 8-eight ounce glasses of water per day. And don't forget to exercise.

5. Maintenance- Begin an appliance folder or folder for warranties, immediately after purchase. Staple important documents together such as receipts that can easily be lost to the inside of the folder. Designate by color-coding, so you can find easily. Plan regular maintenance checks. Make note on the calendar.

6. Record Keeping-One year at a time. Make new folders each year for those accounts necessary. Since most records for tax purposes go back for seven years, it is not necessary to keep twenty years worth of some records.

7. Needs List- Keep a separate list for adding items that pop up as needs. Deal with them on a daily basis i.e. need a battery/night light bulb/ nut for bolt/ pick up dry cleaning, etc. etc.

Academics

"Study to shew thyself approved as a workman who correctly handles the Word of truth." The Bible is the foundation for all knowledge. The application of this knowledge is called Wisdom. The purpose of academics should not be for useless memorization or the acquisition of a vast pool of knowledge for a simple piece of paper called a certificate or a degree.

Making Memories

Take pictures and create family photo albums together and or decorate the home with family photos. Start family traditions (make up your own and/or follow something traditional from your family backgrounds)

- Listen-Truly listen. Restate what you heard to see if it was correct.

- Discover. Seek to understand one another. Listen, learn and accept one another's language of love. Learn to support and encourage each other through good and bad times

- Establish the mood. Playing soft praise & worship music, classical music, using aromatic scents and candles create the sense of peaceful tranquility.

Decorating the Home

Take the time to work together as a couple to decorate your home. If the funds are low, you can find many creative ways to produce a beautiful home. The fun part is working together. Allow the children to take turns setting the table. Children can be very creative with flowers, toys or card arrangements.

Favorite Recipes

1. Follow the Good Book

Follow it line upon line and precept upon precept, the B I B L E.

2. Recipe For Successful Marriage

Ingredients:

3 cups - Tenderness

1 cup - Commitment

1 cup - Consideration

1 cup - Courtesy

2 cups - Unselfish support

2 cups - Milk of human kindness

1 gallon - Faith in God and in each other

Add	1 Cup Each:
2 cups - Praise	Confidence
3 cups - Cooperation	Encouragement
1 small pinch of in-laws	Supportive friends
1 realistic financial budget	Blindness to each other's fault's
3 T pure extract of "I am sorry"	Individual interests and hobbies
2 cups of open and honest communication	

Mix In: Mix in several mutual activities and hobbies. Flavor with occasional tokens of your love and a dash of happy memories. Stir well and remove any specks of temper, jealousy or criticism. Sweeten well with a generous portion of love and keep warm with steady flame of devotion. Never serve with a hot tongue or cold shoulder.

"Stand together yet not too near…let there be spaces in your togetherness…fill each other's cup but drink not from one cup…remember, the oak tree and the cypress do not grow in each other's shadow." Author Unknown

3. **Basic Bread Dough**

4 cups warm milk or water

2 tablespoons yeast

1 teaspoon salt

1/3 cup oil

1/3 cup honey

8 cups freshly milled flour

4. **Plain Pie Pastry**

2 cups sifted flour

1 teaspoon salt

2/3 cup shortening

5 to 7 tablespoons cold water

5. **Mom's Apple Crisp** by Sharon Thompson

5-6 cups apples (cored & peeled)

1 tsp. cinnamon

1 cup sugar

1 cup flour

1 tsp. baking powder

3/4 tsp. salt

1 egg

Place apples in the bottom of 11 x 7 baking pan. Mix together cinnamon, sugar, flour, baking powder, salt, and eggs. Pour mixture on top of apples and then pour 1/3 cup oil over all. Bake at 350 degrees for 30 minutes

6. **Bean Soup**

2 cups mixed dry beans

2 tablespoons salt

2 quarts water

1 lb Sausage (browned) or

meat of your choice

1 large onion

1 clove garlic

1 teaspoon chili powder

1 quart of chopped tomatoes

2 tablespoons of lemon juice

Rinse beans, cover with water, add salt and soak overnight. Drain. Add 2 quarts of water and meat. Simmer for 2 1/3 hours. Add remaining ingredients the last 15 minutes.

Let Love rule!...Kindness was on her tongue

Jacqueline & Betty Ann Lifsey

Chapter 23

The Teen Years

"...For attaining wisdom and discipline;
For understanding words of insight;
For acquiring a disciplined and prudent life,
Doing what is right and just and fair;
For giving prudence to the simple,
Knowledge and discretion to the young-
Let the wise listen and add to their learning,
And let the discerning get guidance-
For understanding proverbs and parables,
The sayings and riddles of the wise,
The fear of the Lord is the beginning of knowledge,
But fools despise wisdom and discipline."
Proverbs 1:1-7

"How can a young man keep his way pure? By living according to your word."
Psalm 119:9

"Flee the evil desires of youth,
And pursue righteousness, faith, love and peace,
Along with those who call on the Lord out of a pure heart."
2 Timothy 2:22

I opened up the refrigerator to see the plate of chocolate chip cookie bars covered with Saran wrap. I couldn't help but laugh when I saw the white sheet of paper with a skull and cross bone artistically drawn with the message "DO NOT TOUCH MICHAEL!" Thirteen-year-olds Janet and Jennifer must have been concerned that their brothers would devour their sweets destined for the Keepers At Home meeting the next day. Oh the teen years....

"Jennifer! Jenn-ni-ferr! You know better than that," I said. She was headed up the stairs as I was headed down. I turned back around to get a quick look at her attire. "Where have I gone wrong? I said out loud as I buried my face into my cupped hands. "What is it Mommy?" she asked innocently, now standing at the top of the stairs. "I put on a skirt like you told me to." "Yes, I can see that." I shook my head at the wrinkled blue skirt and the wrinkled mustard yellow colored sweatshirt. "Jennifer, did you know that they invented irons a long time ago?" I asked. Her mouth turned upward as she broke into a smile. "But Jennifer, that is NOT the problem," I paused, "the problem is that just because you cannot see the dirt on the back of that sweatshirt, doesn't mean other people won't!" She couldn't help but grin, as she realized that I caught on to her little trick of flipping the front of the sweatshirt to the back. It was covered with dirty finger marks and grime. "But I LIKE this shirt!" she said. "Then wash it!" Oh, the teen years…

Janet became frustrated when Jennifer's sewing work did not meet her standards or expectations. As the conversation heated up between the two, I overheard this heated discussion follow, "That's foolish!" one of the girls said, you could hear the other gasping for air. "Auuww!" you're in trouble, you're in danger of the gates of hell if you call me a fool." "I didn't call you a fool," said the other. "Anyway, it's if I say "Raca!" and I didn't say "Raca!" "Yes you did!" "No, I didn't!" "Girls! Girls!" I interrupted…Oh the teen years!

One day the boys remarked on the volume of mail we received. "Hey Michael, do you know why Mommy gets so much Wildlife and Nature Conservation mail?" Mark asked with that little gleam in his eye. Michael didn't answer but gave him the raised eyebrow look. "It's because she saw logs at night when she sleeps. She's using up the forest!" Grrrrrrrrr….Oh, the teen years!

"Hey Janet, this dessert tastes terrible!" Chomp! Chomp! "You could actually hear the chewing sounds he was deliberately making with his mouth. "I'm sure nobody else will want any of it!" Chomp! Chomp! "I'll finish it up for you so no one has to suffer." Mark said. Chomp! Chomp! Oh the teen years!

Ringggg! Rinnnggg! "Hello Mom, I made it to school, may I go to the library after classes?" Michael called to let me know he arrived safely for his college classes. This was his first trip out alone in the car since receiving his driver's license at sixteen. "No son," I answered, "I need you to come home after classes and give me a ride to the store. "Oh," he said.

(Later that afternoon) Rinnggg! Rinnggg! "Hello Mom, I can't come home. I left my car lights on and the battery is dead..." I waited for a moment not sure of what to say. I decided to allow it to be his first lesson in learning how to deal with that kind of a situation. "Maybe you could find one of the student and ask them to give you a jump start." When he returned home that afternoon, he told his brother the story. "I left the radio on, the defroster on and the lights on." Mark couldn't resist it, "Michael, the only thing you didn't do was leave the engine running...." Oh, the teen years...

Oh the teen years! These were the years for continuing training established in the younger years. These were years for teaching them how to succeed through hard work and consistency. These were the years leading to independence and responsibility. Each member of our family from Dad to Mom to the children, had needs that were changing rapidly. Our children were changing physically. There bodies and their behavior were showing signs of hormonal changes. They were developing skills in speaking and communication that were reflective of the time spent among adults and a wide variety of home schoolers. They were not talking back, but they were challenging us in our thinking and beginning to articulate their own beliefs. They were learning to relate to the opposite sex at all ages. They were visiting the nursing home. They were volunteering at a ministry for the homeless and working to build a home with Habitat for Humanity. They were playing basketball and soccer through the community, two local Christian schools and their own arranged soccer team. They were performing various jobs in the neighborhood like dog sitting, horse sitting, or whatever a friend needed done. They were earning money as incentive instead of stars or stickers for a chart. They mowed lawns for our yard, friends and neighbors. The boys' spackled walls and painted ceilings. They worked on mowers and on our cars. They repaired fences and cared for our animals. They helped to write out the check to pay our bills, in order to help give them the taste of reality of the cost of running a home and taking care of a family. They assembled our garage door opener and installed it. They demolished an old shed for a neighbor and an old rotting wooden bridge. Then they along with their father helped to rebuild it.

Continuing Training: Hard Work & Consistency

During the teen years, Michael and I struggled to keep abreast of activities that coordinated with their needs, while at the same time trying to address our own. We poured over educational and college catalogs exploring with the children their options. We visited local colleges and universities. We took the children to job fairs to give them an idea of job fields available. We tried to introduce them to adults in their field of interest so that they might be able to gather information to make a wise decision in the selection of a vocation or occupation. Eventually, the Lord opened the door for Michael to attend a local Christian college at the age of sixteen. He also answered prayer for Mark to be able to attend a military school for two years to complete his Junior and Senior year of high school. Jennifer and Janet were blessed with the opportunity to attend a small Christian school that catered to home schoolers for one year. The next year at the age of sixteen, they entered college.

During the teen years, we found it helpful to be members of a support group. We found that word of mouth was a great way to find out information of services to meet our specific needs for that age group. Information such as where to go for SAT testing or how to sign up for Driver's Ed through the local school or info about the local colleges and universities or classes formed by other home schoolers.

During the teen years, it didn't take much to start a group activity. For example, a few mothers and daughters got together to form a girls' club-called Keepers At Home. Each month the girls would come together to learn various topics such as cooking, sewing, or creative memories photo displays, etc. The girls learned leadership skills. They learned to barter for services with one another.

During the teen years, we tried to prepare our children for working outside of our home. Our son Michael taught piano lessons to several families. On some days, he had 17 students revolving in and out of our house at 30-minute intervals. He was required to keep a record of receipt of payment and a notebook for each student. He wrote out their weekly lessons for them. During this time, the mother of one family taught sign language to our daughters Jennifer and Janet. With each different family that came into our home, we learned various skills and received exposure to their worlds.

141

During the teen years we were able to hire tutors to teach subjects that we felt incapable of teaching or did not have time, like Sign language, Spanish, Art, Biblical world view or voice lessons.

During the teen years we discovered our great error in allowing our teens to parent the younger siblings. Now this was not an intentional thing. We needed their help. Yet we found that our teens were not as patient or as careful as we would have been at times. Then there were times when they were our salvation and more patient than we were at the moment. We found it frustrating that the younger boys picked up quite quickly by example what they saw older children do and say, both good and bad.

Continuing Training: Independence & Responsibility

During the teen years, we really concentrated on preparing for adulthood. We prepared them as best we could through numerous life experiences and courses like the Charm Course for young girls and the Man in Demand for the boys. We studied Christian character as a family and read the Bible every day.

During the teen years, we found that it was important for the teen to see the goal and purpose for what and why they should do something rather than them being made to do it without question. We found it equally important to work from the team approach as we sought solutions to problems.

During the teen years, we discovered that we needed them! In fact, we began to become dependent upon them because each of them had gifts and talents in areas that we did not. Michael and I were moving from labor, task force (where we did most of the work when they were younger) to the managerial position (delegating). Dad was CEO of our home and I (Mom) was the office manager, keeping up bills, filing, school records and the home. Michael Christopher had become the expert in piano and computer knowledge. He helped his Dad and I with forms or accessing information on the web. Mark was our strategist. He loved to study military books of all types. He also had a keen insight into the finest of details with the things of nature. He was the person we called when we found a stray bird, raccoon or snake. Janet was the whiz at cooking, sewing and creating masterpieces of creative artwork. Jennifer was merciful and patient. She was the reader, usually huddled somewhere with a book.

During the teen years, our children learned reality from their experiences in our home. At one point during our home schooling years, we raised animals. The children belonged to a program in our community called 4-H. In this wonderful program, they learned many facets concerning the care of animals. The children were responsible for feeding the animals (lots of 50 lb bags of feed and heavy bales of straw and hay). We learned survival skills as a family, such as how to slaughter animals like chickens, turkeys, sheep and goats.

During the teen years, they were responsible for the care of their younger brothers and they often times would baby-sit for other families. In the future, they will not fanaticize or romanticize having a baby, setting up a house or getting a job. They will know firsthand that being home all day requires an enormous amount of energy and effort, sometimes seeming beyond one's ability to endure at times.

Mark

Michael C. Cross with thirteen of his piano students

Michael, Mark & Nik Sutton visit Wright Patterson Air Force Base

Mr. Nathan Jones teaches the Christian Worldview at the home of the Hockers

Mrs. Glenda West teaches Spanish to Janet, Jennifer, Mark, Amy, Kevin, Mark

Some of the greatest lessons I (Mom) learned were in the teen years when God used my children to teach me. One Saturday morning my 14-year-old daughter Janet came downstairs and asked what she could make for breakfast. "Look at the menu," I said. "It says left over pizza, but since we didn't do the pizza yesterday, we don't have any left over," she answered. "O.K., you're right," I said, preoccupied with what I was doing. "How about pancakes?" she asked. "That's a good idea!" I said as I went on preparing my plate of broccoli with a microwave potato on the side. She pulled the pancake box from the shelf and followed the recipe. She tossed the batter-covered bowl into the sink and grabbed for the refrigerator door. "Do we have any margarine?" she asked "I need it to grease the pan so the pancakes won't stick." She was practically talking to herself, because I was busily trying to finish my notes for an upcoming seminar. She searched around until she found a stick of margarine. I could hear the sizzle as she swirled the margarine stick around the pan and it began to melt. I knew things weren't going well when I glanced around the computer and saw the first pancake break in half. Then the second one broke into several pieces, now she became discouraged. "I don't want to do this anymore!" she snapped. "But Janet, I spoke up now empathizing with her plight," you wanted to do a good thing by fixing breakfast for everyone. Just because it's not turning out the way you want, is no reason to quit." It was then that the Lord spoke to my heart. In my own life, here I was smack dab in the middle of a situation where as an adult, things weren't going the way I planned. I was ready to throw in the towel and just give up. God was dealing with me and speaking to my heart.

I glanced over at the batter. I reasoned from my years of pancake making that the batter was just a slight bit too thick. I also reasoned that if they were falling apart, two egg whites were needed in the batter to hold it together better. I noticed the temperature setting of the electric skillet was just a slight higher than it needed to be since the pan was smoking. "Janet, if you'll add two eggs whites, a little water and turn down your heat, I think you'll find the pancakes may turn out like you want." With downcast shoulders, she trudged over to the refrigerator for the eggs. As she added them, I left my work at the computer and joined her in the kitchen. I added the necessary water and lowered the temperature. After mixing the batter again with the wire whisk, she was ready to pour her third pancake. Together we watched and waited for the bubbles to appear and the sides around the pancake to turn brown, I spoke softly to her. "Janet, just because things don't turn out the way you

146

want, that's no reason to quit. I could hear the words coming out of my mouth to her but in my spirit the message made a boomerang entrance to my own ears. I knew God was speaking to me. "Sometimes Janet, we need to alter what we're doing. Sometimes we need to lower the heat, sometimes we need to add water, or sometimes we need to add eggs. She turned over the perfect pancake. "Janet?" "Yes Mommy," she answered, "How do you think I knew what to do to make that batter better?" "Experience?" she asked with a puzzled look on her face. "Yes, Janet. I have failed many times. But with each time I failed, I learned how to do it better."

I walked away from the stove saying, "Praise you God! I marvel at your ways. I marvel at the way you can use the most simple of illustrations to teach such powerful truths. Thank you for loving me enough to teach me. I praise you God!"

The teen years taught me the folly of getting up late and missing opportunities. When I would go to wake our teenage girls or boys an hour after I had already gone to rouse them, I realized how God must feel when He awakens me to get started on my day and I remain in bed wasting precious time that could be better spent.

The teen years taught me how to better understand the great commission of Jesus. When He left this earth, He promised to send a comforter, the Holy Spirit. He told us to go into all the world and preach the gospel. When I needed to leave the house, I always left them with instructions that I expected to be followed. I didn't do this because I was a tyrant, but I did this because these jobs needed to be completed in order for us to accomplish the goals for the day…

During the teen years, while cleaning up a room one day, I found this little dialogue between Michael and Jennifer. He was in the middle of his first year of college:

Michael: "It's just like you (girls) to go on and on…. nothing outlasts the energizer. Matt and Micah frustrate me beyond belief because I cannot make them obey or cooperate. I get frustrated when I come home and see the house a wreck and Mommy in the kitchen. I guess I am being selfish because I don't consider the work that you might have done. I am not home to see the work you guys do, so I do not know. I do know that Mommy is constantly asking you to do this and to do that and it seems to me that the work is not getting done. If it were, why would she be asking? This frustrates me, because it frustrates Mommy, who cannot manage the household well if things are not getting done."

Jennifer: "You are right! I do go on and on. I'll make this short. I guess it is hard to see. Anyway, it's just that sometimes I don't get the things that Mommy needed done because it just seems silly to do something that is just going to get messed up or ruined or because my standard is not always as high as hers. Hers is almost set on perfection. Sometimes I just feel like talking back to Mommy and standing up for us because she goes off on how we should treat the little boys with love and kindness because if we keep criticizing they'll learn to criticize but then she turns around and does it to us. I know that's rude but sometimes it's like I feel compelled to speak up…. Maybe I'll be a lawyer… What about you? Do you like it there? Is it hard to come home? Do you like it better than home, be honest?" (Sheesh, I meant to write shorter. Oh well, I guess I write my letters too long, yeah, that's it!)

Michael: "You are a female-I expect it! When I come home, I would like it to be a place where I can rest. But lately it seems that I am not appreciated. I know I have been cocky and annoying and I have tried to stop. But I do not like it when people tease me about college. I like to be there and to make friends but I also like to come home and be with my family.

About Mommy…you need to try to understand the pressure she undergoes each day. Observe the things that happen around her and things that she does. Do a little detective work. You will find that she is not as hypocritical as she seems. Think about how you would feel in her position. I know I sound more and more like an adult, condescending to you. I don't mean to be that way. I am only 17 years old, not 20 or 21. Just because I am in college does not mean that I am an adult yet!"

I was tickled to find and read this little dialogue between Michael and Jennifer. Our children were growing up and we needed to make some adjustments during these teen years.

Some of you parents are just like my daughter Janet with her pancake story. You have a lot of failing, learning, practicing, and growing to do before you will find out how to do it well; home schooling takes time even in the teen years. During the teen years, we did not accomplish everything we had planned. We planned to take them through Larry Burkett's financial planning, but we never made it! Life became too hectic! We planned to take them through the Basic Child Training book by Richard Fugate in preparation for their own homes, or at least have them read it in their high school years as preparation. But once college classes began and the school workload took over, there was no time for doing or teaching some of the other things we wanted to impart. These were the things we found we had to leave at the feet of Jesus.

During the teen years, we found that there was still need for correction at times. We noticed as our teens became more involved with their school work and due to their exposure to the outside world, they became somewhat swayed by the philosophies of their peers, instructors or their own self-confidence... They still required our time and attention.

During the teen years, I (Mom) found myself doubting. I would doubt that we had done the right thing by home schooling or doubt our abilities to go any further in higher education. I never felt like we covered enough or that the children had mastered all that was important.

In conclusion, the teen years went twice as fast as the younger years. These years were great years for continuing training for teaching hard work, for leading toward independence and responsibility. These years were great years for growing up together in our relationships with one another and with those outside of our family.

Chapter 24

Seeking Help Outside of the Family

"Therefore let everyone who is godly pray to you
While you may be found;
Surely when the mighty waters rise,
They will not reach him.
You are my hiding place;
You will protect me from trouble
And surround me with songs of deliverance.
I will instruct you and teach you
In the way you should go:
I will counsel you and watch over you."
Psalm 32:6-8

Help For Michael Christopher

There came a time in our home schooling adventure when we felt like there was nothing more we could give our son from home. We had been on enough field trips and covered enough material. Our son was at a level in some subjects that he needed more expertise. We had a choice of working under an umbrella program of a local Christian school or sending him to college. We decided college was a better option to accomplish his educational goals.

Help For Mark

It seemed kind of strange to be sitting there in the lobby of a Columbus hotel waiting for someone whom I had never met. Months earlier, I arranged by phone to meet with Dr. Sutton to do testing for Mark. He had advertised his services in our state home school organizations' newsletter. Mark and I left the house early for the hour and a half drive from

Xenia, Ohio to Columbus. Mark was not happy about this testing adventure. He had better things to do with his time. Dr. Sutton had flown in from South Carolina to meet with several families. I felt assured of his competency from reading his book <u>Strategies for Struggling Learners</u> and from his own personal experiences with his children. He was also an educator from a reputable school.

Mark was obedient, but resistant. At home, he was becoming angrier, and uncooperative in doing his schoolwork. He just seemed to struggle through it. He walked with shrugged shoulders as we met together introducing ourselves to Dr. Sutton. We walked towards the elevators to go to one of the rooms designated for testing. Dr. Sutton made us both feel right at ease. He spoke to me first then he handed me some papers to fill out. While I filled out papers, he began to speak with Mark. He was warm, friendly and a very "down-to-earth" kind of person, so it wasn't long before Mark was happily talking and sharing with him.

I remained in the room while he administered a variety of test with Mark. As he spoke to Mark, his verbal and body language was positive and upbeat. I could visibly see Mark's body language improving with each minute. I noticed several times during the testing that Dr. Sutton acted surprised or commented that he had not seen anyone finish the test so quickly. With each bit of encouragement, Mark seemed to grow in his confidence and ease at being there. I did not know if Dr. Sutton were purposely making these comments to encourage Mark or if he was saying them because they were really true.

At the end of the session he called me out into the hallway to speak privately. Do you know what his IQ is, he asked. "No, I do not," I answered. He went on to explain to me the range that Mark's intelligence quotient fell in. I was both surprised and pleased. In spite of Mark's academic struggles, Mark had a high I.Q. As he explained the rest of the results with me, the picture became clearer. I had made the mistake of identifying a weakness in Mark's learning and was continually pounding him in this area not allowing him to grow in the areas of his strengths and encouraging him to pursue those.

This gave me new insight into the way Mark's brain processed information and helped me to understand myself. I now understood my child better and the path that we now needed to take. I was able to develop an Individualized Education Plan (IEP) that required both remedial work to acknowledge his weakness in an area called a specific learning disability and a way to tap into his area of giftedness.

Mark had always had an interest and love of airplanes. We ordered magazines on flight. We signed him up for Civil Air patrol. We tried to help him in every way we could to open his eyes to his potential. We got him on a basketball team during winter and soccer in the summer. I stopped beating him down verbally in the area of his weakness.

We prayed for wisdom. One day we received an invitation to a friend's retirement ceremony. The speaker was a retired general from the Air Force who now headed up an all boys' school in Virginia. When he described the school to us, the teaching style of the school it sounded just like our unit studies approach in our home school. This school taught one subject for seven weeks, totally immersing a student in a subject and incorporating a mandatory study time each evening. In between time was utilized for extra curricular activities. After receiving a video, looking over the courses offered and the opportunities it would provide, God opened the door for Mark to attend.

God provided Fork Union Military Academy for Mark's junior/senior year of high school. God provided other things for Mark to learn outside of our home and other role models for him to follow. Mark went from being a demotivated student at home, to being an exemplary student there at school. At the award's ceremony, Mark received a scholarship to attend the United States Air Force Academy, a scholarship valued at $225,000.

Help For Jennifer & Janet

God provided Dominion Academy of Dayton, a very small Christian school for them to attend for one year. They were able to study more in depth with instructors in various subjects. Now they had a Biology teacher, an Algebra teacher, a Religion instructor, and an English teacher. The following year they attended Sinclair, a community college.

Help For Matthew

We had home schooled for several years before we adopted our son Matthew. Our bookshelves were full of books collected as we taught the older four children. I was excited and looking forward to teaching him. I was familiar with learning styles and comfortable with our childrens' individual learning paces, but I was not at all prepared for a child with multiple problems.

When we first held our sweet bundle of joy in our arms, we never realized the difficulties that lay ahead. He had a foot that was turned in, a clogged tear duct and a bad eye infection plus he was exhibiting the symptoms of asthma. The doctors called it reactive airway disease because he was so young. We were not prepared for all of the changes his little life brought, but we allowed the daily adventure to be part of home schooling. We were not prepared for all the trips to the emergency room for epinephrine shots. We were not prepared for a child that wanted to be with me all the time. We were not prepared for a child that refused to be left alone or that threw all of the toys out of his crib. We were not prepared for a child that did not listen nor respond to discipline. We were not prepared for a child who was always hungry. We were not prepared for a child that talked incessantly as he grew up. These changes created tension in our home.

My quiet, peaceful home eventually turned into a war zone. The older children had been taught obedience, yet they watched Matthew break all the rules. From their perspective, they saw him getting away with things. Daily life became a war of the wills. It became a war for me to control my emotions. It became daily spiritual warfare. It became a war of the wills trying to get this child to simply OBEY!

I kept trying to make allowances. Maybe he was adjusting to his surroundings; maybe it was all of the asthma medication or the trips to emergency room for epinephrine shots. Maybe the medication was affecting him. I did not want him to feel he was any different from the rest of the children. Maybe, maybe, maybe. I drove myself half-crazy trying to figure things out and keep the love flowing in directions.

I prayed, I cried, I rebuked demons… then the Lord showed me several other mothers with natural children who were having similar or the same exact problems. I was at my wit's end. I was so frustrated that I began to respond out of that frustration. I went from being a calm, peaceful, loving person to being totally frustrated most of the time. I began to inwardly resent my husband because I wanted him to do something. I wanted him to rescue me…I wanted him to take more of an active part in loving this child. It wasn't that he didn't, he tried to show it. But his tolerance level was much less than mine.

Enough was enough, I needed help. As a home schooler, I feared seeking help. I feared intrusion by public authorities. We had been warned many times through the years in home schooling literature about not calling attention to ourselves. But none of those people were in my home nor did they have to endure what we did. We sought help.

I fought labels for so many years. I did not want our child's potential to be limited by a label. So I avoided the ADHD, ADD, Hyperactive labels. But it was not until I sought medical help that I realized the label or I should say the definition or diagnosis that helped me the most. One of the child psychiatrists on the staff of the mental health clinic gave me a handout to read. It described many other mothers just like me, who fit my description and Matthew's profile.

This was not a problem that was just between Matthew and I, nor was it something "I" was doing wrong, it was "the condition." It took a year of me going back and forth to the doctor to realize that medication for Matthew would give our family some relief, especially me. It also helped him to settle down and concentrate. I hated the thought of medicating my child, but our family could no longer tolerate his outburst of inappropriate behavior, which was totally out of control. We allowed Matthew to be on Ritalin for approximately two years. It gave us enough time to work on his behavior and my own. Though he was able to concentrate better, the medication made his seem spaced out much of the time. We got tired of the zombie look and decided to try vitamins, minerals, changes in his diet, consistent firm discipline and loving him unconditionally no matter what behavior he exhibited.

Now I knew that God did not make mistakes, so I continued to try and see what God was doing through all of this. Maybe He designed this child this way for a purpose. Maybe this was the result of poor prenatal care or something in his hereditary background or a generational curse or his feeling unloved or hurt from our poor parenting at times. I don't know, all I knew was that our family needed help. Help came in other ways over time and one of those ways began when we joined a church and met other parents struggling in this and other areas. It was comforting to know that we were not alone. Help came when we started a very small co-operative with other families and we worked together to help our children. Help came through friends who took him for an outing to give us a break. Help came through time as he matured and we ushered him into areas of his interest or into an area where he could find success. We tried sports like soccer, bowling, swimming, skating, and football. We tried classes like music and art.

This section on help for Matthew leaves an open ending because God continues to provide help in various ways even today. The bottom line is this: this is your child; you are responsible for him or her; get help when you need it…do not allow the fear planted by some home schooling "experts" to stop you from getting the help your child needs. Seek godly counsel first. Then proceed in faith. God opened the doors for Matthew to receive testing through the public school. A special thank you to Mrs. Bonnie Benge, principal of Cox Elementary School, Mr. Jon Thorn, School psychologist, and Mrs. Jan Williamson, Special Ed supervisor. God provided Summit Academy, a special school for ADD/ADHD children, Ms. Tasha Hairston, and Mrs. Patty Burris especially for Matthew on September 30th, 2001.

Matthew's class at Summit Academy in Xenia, Ohio

Chapter 25

Is It Time To Say Goodbye Already?

"But as for you, continue in what you have learned and have become convinced of,
Because you know those from whom you learned it,
And how from infancy you have known the Holy Scriptures,
Which are able to make you wise for salvation through faith in Christ Jesus."
2 Timothy 3:14,15

"Anyone who loves his father or mother more than me is not worthy of me;
Anyone who loves his son or daughter more than me is not worthy of me;
And anyone who does not take his cross and follow me is not worthy of me.
Whoever finds his life will lose it, and
Whoever loses his life for my sake will find it."
Matthew 10:37-39

"Never will I leave you; never will I forsake you."
Hebrews 13:5

I took the children outside early one morning. We always tried to begin the day with devotions, and this particular day seemed like the perfect one to be out of doors. The dew had evaporated off the grass so we were able to sit down. I remembered the mother bird who had built a nest in the lamp near our front door the summer before and how she had nudged the little bird from its' nest. Our children were growing up. Their needs were changing and our needs as parents were changing also. I wanted an illustration to reflect what I was feeling. Looking out over our front field where the sheep and goats grazed, the front yard not fenced in and the neighbor's adjoining front yard, I could see where they all blended together to produce an acre or two of land. It reminded me of the huge field of the whole wide world and provided an excellent illustration of my point for today's teachable moment.

I had all seven of us to form a circle as we sat on the front lawn. I then isolated a small patch of grass between my two hands. I further reduced the size by pushing back all the other blades of grass to focus on just one blade. I asked the children to tell me what was unique about that particular blade of grass. Inspecting it very closely, they came up with several detailed points about the blade. When they were done, I released my hands and the blade disappeared into the vast number of other blades of grass that covered the front lawn of our five-acre mini-farm.

From this illustration, I launched into an explanation that compared the uniqueness of the blade of grass to each one of them. I explained that during these years of home schooling, we had been able to focus much time, energy, attention and effort on them. But now, the time had come to open their eyes to the reality that as they ventured into the world as teens and young adults, the focus would no longer be solely on them. They would fade into the sea of humanity.

Michael was sixteen and expressing his desire to go to college. He had studied the piano for four years under the tutelage of Dr. Charles Clevenger, Chairman of the music Department of Cedarville College. He spent one-year teaching piano to seventeen students. Through this experience, he decided not to pursue a music degree, but possibly engineering, math or computer science. He felt he was ready for more challenging work. We also felt that he needed the expertise in subject matter that we could not provide for him.

We prepared him for college life by sending him to Summit World view Academy in Colorado Springs. This ministry started by Mr. David Noebel. It was an opportunity to fly alone, travel and explore. He came back charged and fired up to change his world. He was so inspired by other students there and returned with the determination to teach himself how to play the guitar. While there, he excelled and received the Excellence award for demonstrating commitment to excel in knowing and following Christ.

That summer, Michael had the opportunity to attend a two-week MITE program at Purdue University. This program was for minority students interested in engineering. He came back home with a 1st place in Bridge design and an Overall leadership award in the Engineering Design Project.

Michael graduated with other home schoolers at the annual convention of the Christian Home Educator's of Ohio in Columbus.

This ad appeared in the Dayton Daily News:

Congratulations Grads section

Michael Christopher Cross, we are so proud of you! It has been an honor, a privilege and a blessing to learn and grow together these seventeen years of home education. God has been so faithful to us as a family. Like arrows in the hand of a warrior, your father and I release you into a world desperately in need of men with character. Live your life with integrity son. Keep yourself pure in mind and in deeds. Do good to all people. Flee all sexual immorality. Work hard. Make it your ambition to lead a quiet life, keeping busy with your hands. Always remember whom you represent, our Lord and Savior, Jesus Christ, your family, your church & community, your country. We love you Michael!

Your loving parents, Michael & Jacqueline Cross

With reservations about the college experience and exposure, we allowed him to attend a local Christian college. The first year, he lived at home and commuted back and forth to the campus. The second year, he lived in the dorms. During this year, we saw him less frequently, but we did see him each Sunday in church and on some Fridays after his outreach ministry into downtown.

At the end of his second year, we allowed him to go on a six-week mission trip to a family member's ministry. Michael returned home, but he also had a return airline ticket in hand. He had decided that the Lord was calling him to ministry there in Texas. We had no problems with whatever that Lord wanted, but we did have a problem with the decision being made so hastily and without our parental involvement. This was his choice, and his mind was made up.

Our family was so grieved. We had always been so close. We worked so hard to get this child this far. Both Michael and I were heart-broken. We wanted him to finish what he had started. In our thoughts, we beat up on ourselves, wondering what went wrong. Though we tried to communicate with him over a two-year period, he hardened his heart against us.

> **It was never our plan to keep our children home forever. It was our desire to "train up our children in the way they should go so that when they were old, they would not depart from it."**

One day after receiving a troubling message from him, we sent out an e-mail request for prayer. God is so good in that he especially blessed us with two responses. One man offered to intervene and the other message impacted and encouraged us in a very powerful way. This is what it said concerning the school our son had attended: "I am a grad who had a wonderful experience there - the best years of my life! Though things have changed in 20 years, some things have not. For one thing, many kids there have a rough way to go—more than you think get in deep trouble while there, many get kicked out and many more who should don't. For another, college students in general are more "idealistic" than "realistic" and when their ideals of what Christians are supposed to be "clash" with the reality of what some who call themselves Christians are like at a place like this Christian college, it can create a lot of anger and confusion. Though it is a wonderful place filled with many wonderful people, it is also a human place filled with many fallen humans - both students and leadership. My experience back then (and it is probably more true today) is that while many people want to be there to learn and grow, many kids are there because Mom and Dad say if you want us to pay for a college, that is where you will go." They really do not desire to walk with God, and in fact are rebelling against God. And their behavior shows that. Another aspect is that because of its' "private college" status, there are many wealthy students there as well. There's nothing wrong with money, but like everywhere else in life, it seems to be the thing that people use most often to "get somewhere in life and that draws others to them, and its' not always good. I remember an experience I had in one of the departments. Of all places, it made me realize the Christians don't always operate Christianly! Another fact: I never heard so much garbage, secular rock-n-roll music in my life until I worked at a Christian camp and then attended college with many of those same people!! The bottom line: all the students are very much "in process," and my guess is that at least half of them are not really in touch with God in a personal, life-changing way during that process."

During our oldest son's time out of our home, we were thankful that he stayed with family members, continued his education and worked diligently at a job to provide for himself. About his spiritual condition, we could only pray. Our abiding prayer is that God would heal all hurts and restore our relationships. Now we know firsthand how God must have us on His heart.

Our second son Mark, since childhood, shared a love of aircraft with his father. When we learned of a local Civil Air Patrol group near our home, it was a welcomed activity. Mark was fourteen and his sense of male superiority was setting in. He needed training and education in that area. For several years, Mark learned about military decorum, skills & drills, and leadership. He earned the Amelia Earhart award. Then the Lord provided an opportunity for Mark to go to Fork Union Military Academy. Thank God for General Jackson and his testimony at a friend's retirement ceremony. Mark completed his junior and senior year at Fork Union Military Academy in Fork Union, Virginia. He graduated with honors.

Jennifer and Janet attended Dominion Academy in Dayton for one year. A home schooling pastor and his wife to specifically meet the needs for the difficult years of the upper grades opened this school. The following year, they entered Sinclair College. They were able to complete their junior and senior years of high school and get two years of college under their belts.

It was never our plan to keep our children home forever. It was our desire to "train up our children in the way they should go so that when they were old, they would not depart from it." We wanted them to be prepared to enter their world as mature adults ready for responsibility. Each family must be thinking about, planning for, and adjusting to when the children leave home. It is a fact of life. It will happen at some point. It comes so quickly! Each family must figure out how you're going to deal with it before you're in the midst of it. Learn to be content with the time God has given you to together as a family. Do not beat yourself up with the "what if's." Take today and go forward. Do the things you meant to do or wanted to do whenever the chance presents itself - today! Each family must trust God to fill in the gaps. He is more than adequate.

Graduation Day with Christian Home Educators of Ohio in Columbus

Part
Two

The Challenging Years
of Home Educating

Chapter 26

Sin In The Camp

"If we claim to be without sin,
We deceive ourselves
And the truth is not in us.
If we confess our sins,
He is faithful and just
And will forgive us our sins
And purify us from all unrighteousness.
If we claim we have not sinned,
We make him out to be a liar
And his word has no place in our lives."
I John 1: 8-10

"Therefore confess your sins to each other
And pray for each other so that you may be healed.
The prayer of a righteous man is powerful and effective."
James 5:16

From My Personal Journal

Jan 96

I was walking in my upstairs hallway when I glanced over at the family pictures. I saw several of my sisters and brothers and their children and felt an overwhelming sense of being blessed. "Thank you Lord," I said, "You have been so good to our family! I praise you!"

Mar 96

"Oh Lord, I do not understand. I feel so hopeless, so empty, so hurt. My heart is broken. It seems almost unbearable…Lord, I harbor no malice, no bitterness, no hatred. But I do not understand. I never expected to be betrayed in my own home by someone I respected so highly. Lord, you know I've tried to be faithful to you. You know I have not dwelled on evil thoughts or suspicions. I trusted him. Oh God why? Why must all my hopes and dreams for living a godly life as a godly couple and a godly family vanish? You know I have loved you as best I know how. I've tried to read and study your word, to teach my children and to serve others. Where have I gone wrong?

The pain is so great. Father you promised in your Word that your Holy Spirit would be here to comfort me. Where is the Comforter? How can any good come of this? Is this a test? This seems beyond my ability to endure." "Please Lord," I prayed, "Hear my plea as you have so many others. First, please forgive me for all of my sins against you and for having a pity party for myself. 'Seventy-times seven' you say to forgive our brother that sins against you. Second, help me to forget about myself and help others. Help me to decrease so that you might increase. I pray for my husband. I pray for his deliverance from past sins. I pray for his growth as a Christian. I pray for him to be the godly man you designed him to be. I pray that I might respect him, serve him, and be patient with him until death do us part. Please hear my prayer Heavenly, Father, In Jesus Name."

Sep 96

It's taken me over a week to be able to even write about this. My emotions have gone on a roller coaster ride each time I recall the events. Last week, while Jennifer and I worked on getting ribbons attached to her shoes, we overheard a conversation between our seven and three year old sons. The words were so shocking that I stood mesmerized in disbelief. "What did you say," I asked to make sure I was not misunderstanding. "Maybe I didn't hear right, I thought to myself. He clearly and distinctly repeated it. My stomach sank, I felt sick. Over the remainder of the next few hours, the little details unfolded. Our sons had been sexually molested several months before. They had been threatened and sworn to secrecy. I called Michael, at work. He was in a meeting, already sick, shaking and burning up with fever he came home to deal with this tragic ordeal.

Nov 96

O Lord, not a second breast lump…not another surgery…

Nov 96

Tests results show Matthew is slightly mentally retarded…

Jan 97

Carol (my oldest sister) called in the middle of the night to tell me Sheila (my younger sister) was found dead.

April 97

Mommy called to tell me Tommy (my oldest brother) had shot his neighbor….

-The little boys accidentally burned the barn down

-Wild dogs or coyotes attacked and killed several of our sheep, especially our prized ram Lambert

-I felt abandoned by my friends

> ***Though it is our desire to serve God with all our hearts and to live the victorious Christian life, we live in a wicked and depraved world where Satan lives and breathes for the sole purpose of deceiving and ruining the testimony of Gods' saints.***

Lessons Learned

It all seemed too much to bear. Home schoolers are not an elite core of families who are exempt from tragedy or sin befalling them. Our family is no exception. As my husband puts it, "we all have warts." Though it is our desire to serve God with all our hearts and to live the victorious Christian life, we live in a wicked and depraved world where Satan lives and breathes for the sole purpose of deceiving and ruining the testimony of Gods' saints. This world with all of its' materialism and wickedness tantalizes and beckons the saints to get off course. When we Christians are not fully armed and in His word, we are weak and yield to the flesh of our own sinful natures.

Praise be to the God that we serve. He is a loving, merciful, forgiving Heavenly Father. Only He can take from the ashes of imperfection and create beautiful things. Only He can rebuild, restore and rejuvenate life back into broken, lifeless hearts and lives. As I searched the scriptures for answers, there is not one sin that God leaves for us to wonder about:

1. How do we know that Cain killed Abel? (Genesis 4:8)

2. How do we know that Ham saw his father's (Noah) nakedness? (Genesis 9:22)

3. How do we know Lot's daughter's lay with their own father and conceived children? (Genesis 19:30-38)

4. How do we know of Jacob's deception? (Genesis 27:19-29)

5. How do we know that Jacob's daughter Dinah was defiled? (Genesis 34:5)

6. How do we know that his jealous brothers sold Joseph into slavery? (Genesis 37:28)

7. How do we know of Judah and his time with a prostitute (his daughter-in-law, Tamar)? (Genesis 38)

8. How do we know that Moses killed an Egyptian? (Exodus 2:12)

9. Why did God have to write out the Ten Commandments? (Genesis 3 – Exodus 20)

10. How did we know that the Israelites worshipped a calf? (Exodus 32)

11. How do we know that David committed adultery with Bathsheba? (2 Samuel 11)

12. How do we know Amnon son of David raped his sister Tamar? (2 Samuel 13)

13. How do we know that Achan stole from the devoted things? (Joshua 7, 22:20)

14. How do we know of Samson's disobedience? (Judges 13-16)

15. How do we know of Jammes and Jambres? (2 Timothy 3:8)

16. How do we know about Saul's murderous threats against the Lord's disciples? (Acts 9:1)

17. How do we know Ananias and Sapphira lied to the Holy Spirit and lost their lives because it? (Acts 5)

18. How do we know of the great pressures that Paul faced that were so far beyond his ability to endure that he despaired even of life? (2 Corinthians. 1:8)

19. How do we know of the division in the Corinthian church? (1 Corinthian 3: 1-4)

20. How do we know of the conflict between Paul and Peter? (Galatians 2:11)

21. How do we know of the godlessness in the last days? (2 Timothy 3:1-5) "People being lovers of themselves, lovers of money, boastful, proud, abusive, disobedient to their parents, ungrateful, unholy, without love, unforgiving, slanderous, without self-

control, brutal, not lovers of good, treacherous, rash, conceited, lovers of pleasure rather than lovers of God- having a form of godliness but denying its power."

22. How do we know any of these transparent revelations? Because the Bible tells us so!

Why do we share the truth of our pain and hurts? We certainly take no pride in doing so. The reason we share is for those who come after us. We share to warn you of the dangers and pitfalls. We share because there may be one of you who are trapped in a snare of the enemy. There is a way out…. Call upon the powerful name of Jesus! He died for ALL sin. He forgives you! His mercies are new every morning. We are completely under His grace!

I believe Satan unleashed his fury upon our family. He managed to tempt and deceive my husband and our sons. A second lump was discovered in my breast. One of my children was diagnosed as slightly mentally retarded. My sister either accidentally overdosed on prescribed medication or committed suicide. My oldest brother allowed his anger to cause him to sin and shot and killed his neighbor. Any one of those incidents would have been enough for a yearly event to deal with and here we were facing several in succession. Only God knows why. I ached and grieved for a very long time. I cried and prayed alone. There were times I doubted my faith, but eventually, I went back to search the scriptures for answers, here's what I found:

- Our strength lies in our faith. Our faith is worth more than pure gold to God. The fact that we believe in Him and have never seen Him, counts for something! Our faith is in a God who delivers. It is in a God who saves us from many kinds of fiery pits. It is in a God who forgives again and again.

- Our strength lies in our oneness as husband and wife. Our strength lies in the triple bond of fellowship we share as man and wife with Christ as the Head. Our strength lies in our unity as a family.

- Our strength lies in our unity as believers in the Lord Jesus Christ. Our strength lies in our ability to speak the truth in love. Our strength lies in carrying one another's burdens and so fulfilling the law of Christ. Our strength lies in the power of encouragement, even more as we see the Day approaching. One day soon, He is returning to claim His bride, The Church.

- Our strength lies in our ability to persevere. It lies in our ability to get up, to keep moving, to forgive, and to give up our rights to be angry.

- Our strength lies in our denying ourselves, taking up our cross and following Jesus daily.

These will be some of the most valuable lessons we teach in our home schools, as we model before our spouses, our children, our friends, our neighbors, and the world.

Chapter 27

The Bride of Christ

"Husbands, love your wives, just as Christ loved the church
And gave Himself up for her to make her holy,
Cleansing her by the washing with water through the word,
And to present her to himself as a radiant church,
Without stain or wrinkle or any other blemish,
But holy and blameless."
Ephesians 5:25

"Hallelujah! For our Lord God Almighty reigns.
Let us rejoice and be glad and give him glory!
For the wedding of the Lamb has come,
And his bride has made herself ready.
Fine linen, bright and clean,
Was given her to wear."
(Fine linen stands for the righteous acts of the saints.)
Revelation 19:7

A Letter To Focus On The Family

22 June 1998

Dearest Dr. Dobson & Staff,

We were so sorry to hear the news of your stroke, but rejoice that God has ministered healing to you through the doctors, nurses and so many friends.

This is a letter of thanks and one of encouragement. I started it last September (1997). My husband Michael & I want to thank you for your faithful ministry to our family and to those around the world for many years. We especially want to thank you and your staff for their faithfulness. There is no way you would still be going in ministry without much self-sacrifice, spiritual warfare and sheer determination. We know we are long overdue in sending this letter and our appreciation, but we felt it important especially at this time for you to get a tiny glimpse of the powerful influence your ministry has had on others. We encourage you to continue on in the faith even more so now that we see the Day approaching.

Last month, I (Jacqueline) listened intently as your wife Shirley shared so eloquently at the recent Mayor's prayer breakfast here in Dayton. One particular comment she made stood out in my mind. She said, "Jim wonders when the church is going to wake up!" While I agree in part, the Lord brought to my remembrance Elijah. Remember when he felt all alone, yet God had reserved for himself 7000 that had not bowed the knee. There are many who diligently seek to advance the cause of Christ, though it is not always as visible as those in the public arena. I think of the thousands of moms like me who serve in the trenches of home and family life. The daily spiritual battle is incredible and to many folks would be unbelievable, but is very real. I believe the church is beginning to wake from it lethargic slumber. It is time. Jesus is coming soon!

A Blessing In Disguise

Through the years, our family has been blessed many times over by the Focus on the Family programs. Your program has been a regular part of our home school curriculum. We have always tried to pass on those blessings to others. But at this time, I want to share how one program aired about the woman Laurie in the book <u>Affair of the Mind</u> touched our lives. Although our situation was not as severe as she described, there were elements of it that weaved throughout our lives.

Two years ago, my husband confessed to me that he had succumbed to temptation. During a two-year period of his many travels in the military, especially books/magazines in the airport and the television/cable programs in the motel rooms had tempted him. My sense of security and trust were shattered. We had worked so hard as a couple to keep our lives, our marriage, our children and those the Lord called us to disciple going on the right path.

Michael and I had been married for over eighteen years and home schooling for fourteen when I heard a portion of the program about Laurie and her book <u>Affair of the Mind</u>. I sent for the book not realizing the significant impact it would have on my family.

One evening as I lay quietly on the sofa in the study reading <u>Affair of the Mind</u>, I became convicted of my own sins of the past. We both came from homes with loving, caring, hard-working parents. But neither of us had parents who said anything about sex. We were ignorant of the guidelines that our Bible provided. We learned through what the public schools taught, peers, and our own fleshly desires.

For far too many years, I have blamed my husband for being overly interested in sex. But by my own willingness to begin our relationship over twenty years ago in premarital sex, I had opened the door and invited disrespect for my body and our relationship. Because we had violated "God's Best" principle, we spent many years suffering the consequences of that decision. We never really worked through many of the premarital issues that all couples should before entering marriage. We faced these issues as we experienced them in life. This proved to be a very time-consuming, costly but effective way to learn.

While he lay in the living room lightly dozing, I went over and gently woke him. "I'm sorry," I said. "For what?" he asked. "For violating God's principles. I'm sorry for engaging in premarital sexual activity with you prior to our marriage. In my self-righteousness, I have been focusing on your mistakes rather than my own. I have not completely let go, forgiven and moved on." I suppose you're wondering "Why is this woman sharing all of this with me?" Because our country needs to know that God is a forgiving God. He is in the business of restoration and healing.

> *Because we had violated God's Best principle, we spent many years suffering the consequences of that decision.*

Fresh Start

We decided that we needed to begin anew. We had tried counseling once before early on in our marriage and were very dissatisfied with a pastor who used psychology and created more problems for us. As we sought His (God's) direction, He gently led us over the next fifteen years while we grew in the faith and in our marriage. Now eighteen years later, we were allowing God to guide us once again. We agreed to cease any sexual relationship until after our reaffirmation ceremony which was scheduled for seven months later. We began reading Dr. Ed Wheat's Love Life for Every Married Couple. Michael read it years before and put many of the principles to work. He had given many copies of the book away to other struggling couples. I attempted to read it a few times over the last few years, but I was drowning in housework, babies, home educating etc. and didn't find much time to read it.

Now, for the first time in our marriage, we decided to read it together. Chapter by chapter, sentence-by-sentence, word by word we read the book together. He would read a chapter then I would read a chapter. It was amazing to see how we could read the same words but would be impacted by them differently. We made notes in the margin of the book as we arrived at points that we realized we had violated Biblical principles or each other in some way. There were many tears and many regrets. We apologized, we cried, and we rejoiced. It was very hard and time consuming. It took months to work through. But we always praised God for His loving tender care and absolute patience with us. Gradually we were beginning to understand the oneness principle originally designed by God.

As we worked through the book and a number of other books including the Christ Centered Marriage by Charles Mylander and of course your book Love for a Lifetime, God planted the idea of a reaffirmation ceremony. Our first wedding was a simple one at the Sacramento County Courthouse. It was rushed and very small. It did not include Christ. Now we needed to reaffirm our original commitment to each other but this time it needed to include our commitment to Christ before a host of witnesses. The description given in Affair of the Mind was so helpful to our renewal as we thought about the covenant with God.

God Provided

God provided everything. First, I prayed about a wedding dress. I did not want to spend a lot of money so I asked God for help. One day he directed me to a thrift store. As I drove up into the lot, I could see the dress hanging there in the window. I couldn't wait to get inside of the store. I couldn't believe my eyes when I saw how elegant and stately it was. When I inquired about trying it on, I was told that they don't have a dressing room. But for some reason, she had mercy on me that day and said I could try it on in their employee room. *Oh God, I can't believe this!* I thought as I reached around and zipped up the dress which was a perfect fit. I paid the $45 and walked out of the store as if I were in a dream. During those same months that we worked on the Love Life book, God also worked out little miracles for us too numerous to describe.

As we planned for the ceremony, I envisioned a country blue fabric with flowers for my twin daughters to wear as bridesmaids' dresses. I searched the fabric stores for several weeks and couldn't find what I wanted. Then one day, twenty-year-old Tisha, daughter of a friend called. She was planning to go on another mission trip to the Dominican Republic. I had taken her to purchase clothing once before. These clothes would then be left behind in the Dominican Republic for those who needed them. While I drove her around to my favorite thrift stores to look for clothing, I also kept an eye out for what might work for me as bridesmaids' dresses. We were just about to leave the last thrift store when Tisha came over to me carrying her great buys. "Look what I found," she said as she handed me two flowered country blue dresses with brand new price tags on them. They also had another tag labeled "Country Romance." I stood there speechless as Tisha asked "Won't these fit your girls?" I turned the dresses inside out to discover that they were two different sizes. One would fit my larger twin and the other my smaller twin. Just the perfect fit. I was glad that Tisha was there and found them instead of me, because no one would have believed such a thing.

I frequented the dollar stores for wedding flowers. Tisha Sutton worked for a florist and helped me make the bridal bouquet, bridesmaids' bouquets, corsages and boutonnieres. She also donated bows left over from previous weddings and her own brother's wedding. Another friend, Michelle Roebuck, grew flowers in her backyard to fill two barrels with lovely fresh flowers. My mother-in-law and sister-in-law found a silver napkin holder, silver trays and serving platters at a local Goodwill. Can you tell I'm frugal?

As I began to share our wedding plans, I discovered that there were other couples that had also started their relationships wrong. I invited some of them to join us. I was excited at the possibility that God could be starting a revival or a renewal amongst this small group of believers. As I shared this with my closest friends, the women were willing, but the men were not. They were embarrassed, too shy or unwilling to participate.

The Wedding

Initially, we planned only to have our immediate family members present with a local pastor we had befriended. We decided to add a few friends. It didn't take long before our invitation list went from eight to one hundred twenty-five friends, coworkers and neighbors. My husband Michael and our sons Michael and Mark built an arbor and prepared the yard. My thirteen-year-old daughters Jennifer and Janet planned and prepared food for weeks. Eight-year-old Matthew and five-year-old Micah planned their parts too. It was a great testimony to all six of our sons and daughters. It provided lots of opportunity for us to talk about God's best for them in marriage.

On the day before the wedding I needed to find just the right earrings. I was beginning to get a little frantic inside so I stopped momentarily to pray. With only $14 left in cash, I wondered what in the world I could find with that. I walked right out of the store and paused to decide which direction I should go next. I looked directly in front of me and to my delight there stood a little earrings shop. I went inside to find the perfect earrings with matching necklace that I had envisioned. By now, you're either thinking I'm a wordy woman or you've figured out that I want to share with you that God is real He's on the throne and cares about even the smallest of details. God sent angels to attend us. One of them was our friend and pastor Andy Richardson flew in from Virginia to officiate our reaffirmation ceremony.

We share the painful details of our ordeal in the hopes that some other couple may benefit. It is possible to work through the difficult areas in a marriage armed with proper tools and a faith and belief that God's promises are true.

In His Love,

Michael & Jacqueline Cross

Hannah Geist, Tisha & Hannah Sutton

Reaffirmation Ceremony

Jacqueline Olivia Cross

Cherish the Treasure

Word and Music by Jon Mohr
Sung by Steve Green on Find Us Faithful

I cherish the treasure

The treasure of you

Lifelong companion

I give myself to you

God has enabled me

To walk with you faithfully

And cherish the treasure

The treasure of you

As I obey the Spirit's voice

And seek to do His will

I then can see the wisdom of His plan

For as He works His will in me

I then can love you selflessly

And by His grace, can pledge my love

To you

This sacred vow I make to you

Does not contain an "if"

Though I'm aware that trials lie ahead

I will love you and pray with you

And through it all, I will stay with you

Our home will be a refuge of

Unconditional love

Cherish the treasure

The treasure of you

Chapter 28

One Godly Man

"How can a young man keep his way pure?
By living according to your word.
I seek you with all my heart;
Do not let me stray from your commands.
I have hidden you word in my heart
That I might not sin against you."
Psalm 119:9

We were over visiting another home schooling family one afternoon, when just as ten-year-old Matthew, six-year-old Micah and I were about to leave, she asked me if I would pray about something. "We're going out of town and wondered if a young woman from the Crisis Pregnancy Center could stay with you for that week we're gone," she asked. I spoke with Michael about it and my friend brought the young lady over to meet us the next day. While my friend and I chatted, one of my daughters started a conversation with our nineteen-year-old guest and the two of them went over to the piano and began to play piano pieces together. Our daughter Jennifer reminded her of her own younger sister.

Since eighteen-year-old Michael Christopher, our oldest was living in a college dorm room and our seventeen-year-old Mark Anthony, second son was away in a military school, our family felt God calling us to minister to this young woman for the week. It was amazing how quickly seven days passed, but at the end of the week, our guest had become comfortable and wanted to stay.

It was difficult to face our friends who originally allowed her to stay in their home, but as Christian couples, we met together to pray about what was in the best interest of our new young friend in her ninth month of pregnancy. We all came to the agreement that she would move in with us while she awaited the arrival of her baby and for housing. During this waiting period, we tried to prepare her with helpful books, articles, and baby items. She was in the middle of a real dilemma. First of all, I'm sure there was the question "Do I keep this baby?" She was a freshman in college nearing the end of the school year. She already had a 3 year old in foster care in another city. She needed to make weekly visits to maintain her parental rights or else lose custody permanently. She didn't have a car. She didn't have a job. But she had a talent, a beautiful voice. For that, she earned a scholarship. She had a dream to sing opera. She desperately wanted to parent her children. This notion drove her, forced her to push ahead. She believed the system had failed her and this was a miscarriage of justice. All she wanted was for everyone to go away and leave her to love, mother and take care of her children…

For twenty years, Michael and I had been diligently working, day in and day out to prepare our family for living in this world, now here we were, faced with a young woman ill prepared for adulthood. The first thing she needed was a mother figure. Her own mother was many miles away, so the Lord called me to stand in the gap. I recognized from her condition, now in the ninth month of pregnancy, that she and her baby needed good nutrition, sleep and mental relaxation from the stresses of all the decisions.

There were days when I prepared breakfast and laid out the vitamins for her or did laundry. I woke her in the mornings to get her to class on time. I drove her to college classes and sometimes I picked her up. I drove her to doctor appointments. I walked with her, prayed with her and I listened to her. I sat with her, talked with her, cried with her and I listened to her. She was trying so hard. How I desperately wanted her to succeed! But as the days grew into weeks, it became more and more apparent that this young woman could not parent, set up a home, go to school and work-alone.

Within a few weeks, the baby was born and I was there. This was my first time attending the birth of a human being other than my own children. Oh, how marvelous and wonderful to witness the beginning of God's precious gift of life outside of the womb. The baby was adorable and beautiful! As her mommy cradled her in her arms, she did not know of the many strikes against her little life. It was clearly obvious what was missing; one godly man.

As the next six weeks passed, it was clear that what one godly man could have provided, a whole community of people could not. If there had been a godly man, this young woman would not have needed the foster care system. She would not have needed a family to care for her son nor the caseworker, nor the lawyer, nor the court appointed guardian ad lie tem, nor the guards to watch them during their visits. She would not have needed the Crisis Pregnancy Center to provide counseling, maternity clothes, baby clothes or diapers.

She would not have needed the church donations or the WIC program for cheese and milk. She would not have needed food stamps or the Housing Authority. She would not have needed the Mental Health agency for counseling. She would not have needed the rescue squad after an attempted suicide or the staff at the local hospital or the medication or the bills that she could not pay. If one godly father had provided a stable, loving home jointly with his wife for her, had prayed with her and over her during her growing up years, what a difference it might have made. If he had prepared her with character training, academic training, and his complete fatherly love necessary for life upon this earth, what an impact he might have made. If one godly man had been a father to this young woman and then released her into the arms of a godly son-in-love, how he might have impacted generations to come.

One godly man would have taken pride in his god-given responsibilities of manhood. He would have gone to work to provide for his family. Let me tell you about one godly man. He is my husband, Michael Anthony Cross. He is surely one of the greatest men to walk upon this earth. He was born November 3rd, 1955. He grew up in Kingston, Jamaica. He was the first child of an unwed sixteen-year-old. At the age of three, he watched his parents marry. At the age of twelve, he and his siblings were left with relatives in Jamaica while his parents came to the United States to make enough money to bring them over. He entered the U.S. as a fourteen-year-old. He went to school in the Bronx and transferred to Aviation High School in Queens, New York. He attended the Air Force Academy, in Colorado Springs, Colorado for four years and served his country for twenty-one years in the Air Force. He retired with distinction as a Lieutenant Colonel.

My godly man has not been a perfect man, but he has been a faithful man. He has been faithful to love and provide for his family even though unbeknownst to me, the scars of his past had deeply affected him. His molestation as a six year old boy by an older girl and the bad influences of the teen years set in motion a wrong belief system that caused him much internal turmoil and pain. He never allowed that to interfere with our relationship or our children.

My godly man has messed up; he has made mistakes. He has repented of his sins and worked diligently to overcome those things that were once strongholds in his life. He has been faithful to work and to work hard. He works diligently until the end at no matter what he sets his mind to. He is determined. He perseveres when all odds seem hopeless and futile.

My godly man has been faithful to go to church or to lead services in our home. He has taught Sunday classes, coached soccer teams, and extended hospitality many times over in our home. He has watched our children and others without complaining. He has opened up his home and his heart to adopt two children and raise them as his own. He has done the dishes or the laundry or the floor whenever necessary.

My godly man has allowed me to pursue my dreams. He has worked beside me and behind me to accomplish those values I hold dear. He has paid the rent for the apartments and the mortgage for the houses. He has paid for the cars and for the insurance. He has paid for the medical and dental bills, the ballet lessons, the soccer teams, the clothes and for food. He rarely asks for anything for himself.

My godly man has been extremely patient with me, his wife. He has tolerated my adventures and curiosities. He has listened to my 25,000 words per day, whenever he could. He has counseled me and corrected me. He has been by my side during the births of our children and during my illnesses. He has been patient to endure my rejection at times, my anger, and my bitterness. He has truly loved me. I know he would give his life for me or for his children. His value cannot be measured.

> *Why would the enemy want a woman to love, honor, cherish, respect and encourage her man when he knows the incredible power it holds for future generations?*

This is why our enemy, Satan, has worked so hard to destroy the men of our society. This is why Satan will work diligently to destroy your man and your family. Why would the enemy want a woman to love, honor, cherish, respect and encourage her man when he knows the incredible power it holds for future generations? Why would the enemy want a woman to nurture, care for and establish a loving foundation for little boys who will someday become men and hopefully follow in their father's footsteps? Or nurture little girls who will deliver boys and teach to become godly men? He hates one godly man…

(As I wrote this I wept from the depths of my soul. If it were possible to hear the heart of God, I believe His Spirit would wail so loudly and for so long that this world could not contain His tears. He would sob and sob and sob! I believe His Spirit is greatly grieved over His creation today. The degree of wickedness and brokenness can be compared to Noah's day or Sodom and Gomorrah. God is a loving Father. He is a faithful provider. He is a patient, long-suffering, merciful God. His original plan for man never included such heartache as we see now. He loves walking with His children. He loves to love them and to bless them. He loves to teach them, guide them and lead them. He is so gentle and humble. But His duties also include judgment and wrath against the unholy things that sin brings. But even in His anger, there is this complete abiding love…)

Satan, the devil, the Father of lies has not changed:
1 Lust of the Flesh

2. Lust of the Eyes

3. The Pride of Life

He hates one godly man!

Lt. Col. Ret/Michael A. Cross w/Jennifer & Janet

Chapter 29

I Have A Dream Too...

"In the last days, God says,
I will pour out my Spirit on all people.
Your sons and daughters will prophesy,
Your young men will see visions,
Your old men will dream dreams,
Even on my servants, both men and women,
I will pour out my Spirit in those days,
And they will prophesy.
I will show wonders in the heaven above
And signs on the earth below,
Blood and fire and billows of smoke.
The sun will be turned to darkness
And the moon to blood
Before the coming of the great and glorious day of the Lord.
And everyone who calls on the name of the Lord will be saved."
Acts 2:17-21

Dreams of a Resource Center

I went back and forth several times during the week of youth ministry at the Hillside Retirement Home owned by Jim and Mary Lou Preston of Xenia, to check on our teens Mark, Jennifer, and Janet. I marveled at the over 70 youth involved in the week long ministry tour headed up by the youth minister, Mr. Greg Trout of Patterson Park Church in Beavercreek, Ohio. This was the first time that my home schooling children had been involved in a youth activity of this magnitude. They were resurfacing the parking lot, scraping the old paint off of windows, pulling weeds, planting flowers, trimming bushes, and they were making a walking path in a nearby field for the residents of Hillside. In between times, they did Bible studies with the teens, with the residents and visited throughout the neighborhood sharing their faith. At the end of the week, they arranged for a little carnival complete with clowns, popcorn machine, snow cone machine, moon walk, water tank and invited the neighborhood children. As I walked around the facility admiring all that the youth had accomplished, I realized that when they were gone, there would still be work to be done. This was a ministry of service opportunity.

The Lord pricked my heart concerning the opportunity for home schoolers to become involved in a ministry such as this. Home schoolers were always looking for opportunities to put their faith into action. *This facility might serve a twofold purpose*, I thought, *in providing a place for home schoolers to maintain resources and the ministry opportunity for service to the elderly residents of Hillside.* My brain began to tick off the ideas. *Families could select a flowerbed and maintain it as a project. Families could build birdhouses and place them around the facility. Families could come over and choose a resident to befriend and visit routinely. Families could perform their singing or drama acts for the residents,* I thought. Hillside had some available space and several of the newer home schoolers needed a resource center. To me it seemed like a perfect match. After asking Michael about it, I took Sharon, another home schooling mom and we approached Jim and Mary Lou concerning the possibility of using one room for a resource center. To our surprise and through their generosity, they offered us (our home school support group) an entire wing of their building.

It had been a fifteen year long dream of mine to have a resource center where home schooling families could have access to a wide variety of home schooling curriculum, other experienced home schoolers, more educational helps, copy machines, a laminator, computers, field trip information, and networking information. I had struggled in these areas most of my home schooling years and had seen other families struggle as well. I particularly wanted to see others who chose to home educate, prosper and succeed. Our family wanted to be a blessing since we knew how hard it had been for us in the home. Mothers especially, as primary teachers in the home, need a place to retreat or a place to think, plan, and prepare. We envisioned a self-help resource center where the members or newer home schooling families could come to begin their journey or have access all year long to materials of interest to home schoolers. We hoped to have complete sets of traditional curriculum and whatever else we could find for families to view before purchasing. We hoped other more experienced home schooling families would join us and share from their wealth of experiences. The Lord used my brother Pastor Charles H. Ware Jr. to show us the possibilities when we were able to make a visit to the Home Dome in San Antonio, Texas.

This facility was a converted skating rink, which housed a bookstore, basketball court, and classrooms for home schoolers. We also visited a resource center ministry started by Harvest Presbyterian under the direction of Mr. Eric Wallace in Virginia. We were so excited, full of hope and dreams.

> Mothers especially, as primary teachers in the home, need a place to retreat or a place to think, plan

We invited our support group to check out the Hillside facility to see if it were of interest to them. Though God had laid the vision on our hearts, we knew it was a gift from Him to them. We greatly valued any input, suggestions or donations. We felt blessed that He would call us to this work. We also felt frustrated and baffled. At first, the members began to donate and visit the facility. Within a few months, through miscommunication and a deceptive work of the enemy (Satan hates for good works to be accomplished), things began to change. Changes were also occurring in technology (what was available through the Internet) and in the educational systems (with the advent of Charter schools) and amongst local support groups. We continued to work. We spent one year making resources and ourselves available to help home schoolers get started. We spent the second year helping families in practical ways learn how to co-op teach with other families, share materials, pool resources and knowledge. God is so faithful in that He richly provided for each of the eighteen rooms to eventually be completely filled with furniture, books, and equipment. God is so faithful in that He provided people to be ministered to and through. God is so faithful!

Through His faithfulness, He allowed us to host kinder music classes. He provided a pastor's wife and teacher (Mrs. Krueger) who drove from Cincinnati to teach the children music. Often they would go over to the residents of the retirement home to sing their songs or play their instruments. What joy this brought to the residents! An Air Force wife, Mrs. Nancy Cook taught several families how to weave a basket. Another young home schooling mother Mrs. Diane Phelps brought in her aunt to teach the young mothers and teens how to make lovely place mats for Christmas. A home schooling father Mr. Chip Sutton gathered the men and their sons for Christian Service Brigade. The Resource Center provided a meeting place for them to build strong relationships as they worked together to rake leaves, trim trees or visit the residents. He allowed me to teach Writing Road To Reading classes to help younger mothers in teaching their children basic phonics. He provided Mrs. Lisa Webb, to serve home schoolers by teaching art and guitar lessons. He provided several certified teachers (Mrs. Kim Baird & Mrs. Bonny Williams) who used the facility to go over a families' portfolio for the years' end assessment or for families to do standardized testing. He allowed it to be used as a meeting place for several families to learn how to start a cooperative and to be a place of prayer. He allowed us to make many visitations to the elderly and to glean wisdom.

The residents always loved seeing the children even though sometimes they were fidgety or loud. We received joy in return as we played checkers, worked puzzles or listened. The children represented life. The children represented hope. The children were a reminder to the residents of their own families and of times gone past.

One of the residents named Mary Braden was a calm and gentle woman. I'll never forget the day she headed out of her room in a wheelchair. The children and several of the mothers greeted her. She just returned from the doctor and was quite bothered by the condition of her hands. "May we pray for you?" I asked. We all prayed for Mary. Several months later, she went to be with the Lord. What a sweet memory of that day we have, as the children gathered around her to pray.

Meeting the residents and hearing their stories were life changing for us. Each Thursday afternoon Matthew and Micah would volunteer to sit with the residents to sketch them or play games. One day as I sat with Mabel, Claire, and Helen. I was delightfully surprised with a history lesson. As Helen spoke to Mabel, she told of being the first woman called to teach at Cedarville College (now Cedarville University). "I taught the Pentateuch and Personal Evangelism," she said. "My uncle George Milner was head of Midwest Missions. He asked me to come. My family started the college," Helen said. "Oh," Mabel retorted I thought Jeremiah did. Our family belonged to his church in Toledo. My sons Don and Jimmy work at the college." "Well my daughters Libby and Molly are up there too," Helen replied. "Libby teaches and Molly is at the reception desk." Claire was sitting and listening.

"Claire," I called, "Guess where I've been?" "Where?" she asked in her low voice. "My family and I went to Orlando. We saw all of those lovely orange groves that you told me about." Her face lit up with a beaming smile. Claire had been a resident at Hillside for two years. She loved to tell me about her work with the little children in Sunday school and her forty years of living in Florida. She loved to tell me about her work in the church, her marriage and her heartbreak concerning a son. "My husband was a pastor," Helen started speaking again, "He was very good at organizing churches then starting them up somewhere else. You know my family, the Milner family started Cedarville College." Oh," Mabel responded, "I thought Jeremiah did..."

I also learned that Helen had worked as a teacher in one of the local schools in Xenia for many years. Charles (we called him Mr. White) was a cartoonist for the local newspaper. He often talked about his children (two daughters lived in Xenia and his son in another state). On several visits he shared how he desperately wanted to see his son. Nell always had a smile on her face. She loved to ask the question, "If you died tonight do you know where you'd go?" Then, she would tell you about Jesus. Her husband Troy stayed mostly in his room, and Nell his wife of 52 years stayed close by his side. Clara Bony beamed each time she spoke of her children (Dan & Bernie Sietman of Beavercreek), grandchildren or the little children down in Florida that she taught in Sunday school classes many years ago...What a blessing!

The dream that we had for this resource center for home schoolers to operate just like the New Testament saints from the book of Acts 4:32, did not materialize in the manner which we had hoped. It was heart breaking to see what God had prepared to be a blessing and provision not be utilized. It was difficult to watch blessing after blessing intended for home schoolers to be lost. It was heart breaking to see the Body of Christ amongst home schoolers never realize its' full potential. We pray that in our sharing this, a seed would be planted in the hearts and minds of those who come after us. God wants to bless you! He really, really does! He richly provides!

Though at times, it felt like we failed, God did fulfill the desires of our hearts. First of all, He fulfilled the vision that He had given us. He taught us about prayer, simply talking to Him and telling Him of the needs and sharing with others. He taught us about waiting, trusting and listening to His still small voice. He taught us about persevering and walking alone. He taught us about real, genuine friendship, and how adversity reveals true friends. He taught us about working hard and pursuing the dream, in spite of the tricks of the enemy. He taught us about servant hood, mercy and compassion. He taught us about human nature. He taught us how negative thinking, jealousy, criticism and gossip can destroy quicker than what it takes to build. He taught us that we have much more to give and much more to learn. He taught us about moving on, moving forward, and looking up. He taught us about the principle of the vine and especially the principle of the fruit. "You will know my disciples by the fruit they bear…"

> **He taught us about persevering and walking alone. He taught us about real, genuine friendship and how adversity reveals true friends.**

It is our dream that every parent who chooses to home educate have immediate access to the help they need to begin their journey. It is our dream that every parent should have access to the best possible materials available without regard to cost. It is our dream that curriculum choices, equipment, tutorial services, continuing education classes, student assessment and testing be available exactly at their point of need. It is our dream that older more experienced home educators be available to guide, direct and encourage younger families starting off. We strongly desire to see families succeed and prosper in home education!

We would like to close with this word of encouragement: We hope and pray that families who choose to home educate will learn how to come together to pool their resources, their talents their experiences, and their knowledge. Someone may have a bookshelf to donate, someone else several unused books to donate, someone else may have a talent or a building to donate. You will never know until you ask. You will never find until you seek. You will never succeed or fail until you try. We hope and pray your family will be stimulated as home schoolers to truly reflect the Body of Christ as you work together toward growing mature followers of Christ. We hope and pray your families will think creatively and pursue your God-given dreams diligently! We hope and pray that some day every parent who chooses to home educate will have access to the best available materials for them and their child.

We wanted to say a special "thank you" to those who helped make our God-given dream come true: Jim & Mary Lou Preston, Jody Ames (Dentist), Kim Baird, Jeff & Lora Beam, Kristie Carl, Tim & Kathleen Carroll, Craig & Jeri Carson, Ken & Margaret Colvin, Diane Cope, Kathy Donegia, Bob Eustace, Cheryl Ford, Randy Franklin, Ken & Nancy French, Carol Harlow, Jerry & Joyce Hill, LeAnn Hill, the Hunter family, Sharon Thompson, Libby Pidgeon, Michelle Roebuck, Cathy Johnson, Melissa Knowles, Mary Musselman, Tammy Norckauer, Lynne Riley, Denny and Jeanie Roeck, Sandy & Christopher Samuelson, Ken & Cindy Schumaker, Screenplay Printing (Paper donation), Nelu & Marcie Silaghi, Doug & Sandy Sjoquist, Chip & Rene Sutton, Karen Tucker, Ted & Tina Vanlandeghem, Bill & Lisa Wiedenhammer, Bonny Williams, Debbie Wills, Fred & Gilda Winkler, Wanda Wist (science books and equipment), Bob & Toni Wright. A very special thanks to my husband Michael Anthony Cross (who continually allows me to pursue dreams), to my children (who have always worked diligently by our side) and especially to my Heavenly Father, the dream maker.

Dreams For The Body Of Christ

One evening back in 1981 I was reclining on my bed with my arms crossed and overlapping behinds my head. I was pondering many things. I must have drifted off to sleep because I suddenly became aware that I was in a strange place, somewhere I had never been before. I was walking along in total darkness, yet I was totally aware of my surroundings. It seemed to me that I was walking along narrow alleyways with massive stones all around me. While my mind struggled to figure out where I was, I became acutely aware that I was not alone. Someone was walking beside me. Though in total darkness, I was keenly alert. We began to communicate with our minds, though neither of us uttered a word. This was too bizarre for me and yet I sensed total peace. We walked until we reached a small opening in the stone wall. I remember very distinctly, the square sort of stone curb we stepped over just before we bent down to enter the dark cave. Once inside, He pointed to a pile of gathered cloth on the top of a square stone boulder. Again, I racked my brain trying to figure out what in the world this was all about. Then it clicked who this was, it was Jesus! The moment I realized who He was and turned my head to look at Him, He disappeared. *He's real!* I thought. *Jesus is real and He loves me!* From that moment until today, I have passionately sought to know and understand Jesus.

Most recently, one of my dreams revealed a flat map of the entire world. Super imposed over it was a headless, transparent body with outstretched arms and legs. I could even see the tiny blood vessels and arteries. These represent the Christians around the globe who form His body. The missing head represents Christ. One day soon He will come to claim His bride-the church.

The Heart Of God

I'll never forget the day in the Resource Center when one of the younger mothers came up to me to complain. In her mind, it was a mountain; in my mind it was a molehill. As I stood there trying to understand what message she was trying to convey, I thought about all the work that had been done to provide the building, the materials, even the time to serve home schoolers and others. Yet, all she could see was her own needs, my faults, and whatever other criticism she could find. In a way that only God could do, He made me keenly aware of His presence. I felt such a peace in my spirit. I listened intently for what He was trying to teach me through this experience. He allowed me to experience the moment from His perspective. I truly experienced "the heart of God." In comparison, He had created the world, He had given mankind the breath of life every day, the food to eat, the clothes to wear, the jobs, even the unnecessary wants and yet, all mankind could do was nitpick and find fault with whatever what not going right in their world from mankind's perspective. I felt humbled by the insight, and determined not to be judgmental or critical. I resolved to do what I could to lift up, encourage and serve others.

God's heart is always reaching out to the little lost lambs. He is trying in every way possible to express His love to all of His children. The most devastating part is that many Christians are asleep. Why are they asleep?

> **The reality of the triune God is completed and brought to life through the Holy Spirit working in the earthen vessel called "You." You represent Jesus to the world. You have been sealed until the day of redemption**

1. **Deception by the enemy**: Satan knows his time is short. He is appealing to the "**flesh**." He is appealing to us through sexual immorality/pornography/gambling/ drugs/alcoholism. He is appealing to us through our "**eyes**." He is appealing to us through our "**wants**." "I want more things; I want what I see." He uses material possessions through medians such as billboards, television; newspaper ads; magazines; computers; to draw us in. He is appealing to us through "**the pride of life.**" He is using our jobs, houses, cars, status in life, number of degrees, and accomplishments to entice us.

2. **Ignorance of the Word of God**: The majority of Christians are afraid and cannot share their faith because their knowledge of God's Word is second hand. Many are basing their beliefs on the traditions of a particular denomination, what their parents believed or on what they heard a pastor or speaker say. They can't share because the Word of God has been taken in by the "verse here or verse there" method. Many Christians don't know who they are in Christ (His Child) and what is available to them through Christ Jesus.

#3 **Lethargy/Laziness**: Many Christians are malnourished both physically and spiritually. Many are overeating unhealthy food and forgetting where their true home is. People are literally dying for lack of knowledge, both of the Word of God and the awareness of His Holy Temple-their bodies. People are dying spiritually, emotionally, and physically because the good works God ordained for us to do are not being accomplished. Christians are too busy playing the game of Churchianity, "going to church" instead of living for Christ. Do you wonder why so many are coming up with cancer, diabetes, high blood pressure, heart attacks, depression, divorces, deaths, etc? Do you wonder why so many Christians are falling prey to sin? Most people read a verse or two and expect to understand God. Most do not understand that the whole Bible in its entirety is the **foundation for all life**. The Old Testament reveals God the Heavenly Father-creating, providing, loving, correcting and discipling His children. The New Testament reveals God the Son-Jesus, sent by God the Father as the provision for the sins of all mankind. Upon believing in Jesus and by faith trusting God to honor His promise, we are sealed by the Spirit of the Living God.

The reality of the triune God is completed and brought to life through the Holy Spirit working in the earthen vessel called "**You**." Upon your acceptance of Jesus as Lord and Savior, you become His property. You have enlisted into His army. You represent Jesus to the world. You have been sealed until the day of redemption.

Unfortunately, many Christians neglect Bible reading. Many do not experience true "koinonia" fellowship. This type of fellowship brings us all together as brothers and sisters in the Lord. Many do not understand the spiritual significance of food and how every morsel put into the mouth should be for the nourishment of His Holy Temple. Every ounce of energy produced by that food should be used for the glory of God. It is living a disciplined life.

Most importantly, I believe God wants us to recognize our "**interdependence**." We Christians are His body and we need each other. We seldom speak the truth in love, we lie to tickle one another's ears, but we freely tell someone else the "truth." We often segregate ourselves into little "cliques" as if we are in secret clubs. Then, the message of Christ, which should be shared openly, boldly and courageously with the world, is hushed and held in silence and fear by Christians.

Now, if you think I'm trying to set myself up as a self-righteous, judgmental, pompous, arrogant, whatever word you can think, you're wrong! I know who I am. In my flesh, I am nothing, but dust. But in my spirit, I am His child. I am His daughter and He loves me. I know I am saved for all eternity. I am righteous because of His righteousness. I know that my faith is worth more than pure gold to Him and the fact that I believe in Him without seeing Him, counts for something. I know that I (as part of the universal church) am His Bride. I know I am a co-heir with Christ. I am an heir to the promise given to Abraham. As a Gentile, I have been grafted in and adopted into the family of God. I have been circumcised in my heart. I know I am sealed by the Holy Spirit as a deposit guaranteeing what is to come.

I truly believe God is making every effort to present Himself to mankind, in many ways. We, the universal church need to recognize what is available to us in Christ. Once we do, all we can do is "Praise the Lord!!!!"

It is important to realize that at the core of every human being is a desire to be loved, to be accepted, to have a purpose in life, to want to matter, and to want to count for something! But God does not want us to accomplish this in our own strength. He wants us to recognize that He loved us enough to send His only begotten Son. He wants us to recognize that when we receive Jesus into our hearts, we are accepted into His Kingdom. He wants us to know that He has a purpose for our lives. He wants us to know that our life does count for something, since He gave His life's blood to redeem it. We need to get our perspectives right. This place is not our home.

I do not claim to be a prophet, but I can see very clearly from a combination of Bible reading, revelation from the Spirit of God, life's experiences over the past 45 years on this earth and the troubling condition of our world, that I can boldly speak as one with authority to say, "my message from the Lord is this: *To the lost*, the message from the Word of God is this: **Repent**! For the Kingdom of Heaven is near! **Believe** on the Lord Jesus Christ and be saved!" *To the found,* the message is "**Wake-Up, The King is Coming Soon**! Be about the Father's business."

"He who wins souls is wise…" (Proverbs 11:30)

God is depending on YOU
To get His message through!

Matthew 28:18-20

Jim & Mary Lou Preston of Hillside Retirement Home with Michael & Jacqueline, Matthew & Micah Cross, Megan & Nicolas Norckauer, Christopher & Jonathan French, Sam, Michael & Hannah Roeck

Ken & Nancy French, Michael & Jacqueline, John Norckauer, Denny & Jeannie Roeck, Craig & Jeri Carson

Broken Dreams

Author unknown

As children bring their broken toys
With tears for us to mend.
I brought my broken dreams to God
Because He was my Friend.

But instead of leaving Him
In peace to work alone.
I hung around and tried to help
With ways that were my own.

At last I snatched them back and cried,
"How can you be so slow?"
"My child," He said, "What could I do?
You never let them go."

He heals the broken hearted and binds up their wounds.

Psalm 147:3

Chapter 30

Totally Burned Up

"The Lord God formed the man from the dust of the ground
And breathed into his nostrils the breath of life,
And the man became a living being."
Genesis 2:7

"The high priest carries the blood of animals into the Most Holy Place as a sin offering, but the bodies are burned outside the camp. And so Jesus also suffered outside the city gate to make the people holy through his own blood. Let us, then go to him outside the camp, bearing the disgrace he bore. For here we do not have an enduring city, but we are looking for the city that is to come."
Hebrews 13:11-14

"...It is a burnt offering,
An offering made by fire,
An aroma pleasing to the Lord."
Leviticus 1:17

"Therefore, I urge you, brothers,
In view of God's mercy,
To offer your bodies as living sacrifices,
Holy and pleasing to God—
This is your spiritual act of worship."
Romans 12:1,2

ur barn was engulfed in flames. We all stood there speechless as we watched the mushroom like cloud produced by the mixture of hay, straw and equipment burn. We watched for 15 minutes as five years of our labor went up in smoke. Everything in the barn burned to the ground, even our 1984 mini-van parked next to it. Everything totally burned up and that's how I was beginning to feel inside.

I was 180 lbs. I wanted to sleep every chance I got. I didn't have any energy. I didn't have any desire to do anything. I was burned out from all the years of persevering through 20 years of military moves, parenting six children and home schooling. I was burned out from feeling like I didn't know what I was doing right or what I was doing wrong. I was burned out from trying to figure out what curriculum to use or what activity to become involved in. I was burned out from having to play the role of mother, father, referee, maid, cook, teacher, chauffeur, school administrator, bookkeeper, bill payer, etc. etc. I was burned up from feeling like a failure over several broken dreams. Everything in me, felt totally burned up.

I was burned out from the years of enduring the difficulties of growing up with a mildly mentally retarded child and a hyperactive one. While one child was extremely slow in the brain, the other was extremely fast and got into all kinds of trouble, all day long! One minute, one would lead the other into cutting lines into their hair, or completely cutting the front of it off or maybe they would use the clippers to clip the metal blinds at the bathroom window. Maybe they would get into Dad's shaving cream and shoot it at one another. Or maybe one would throw a toy too hard and knock a hole into the drywall or one would get angry and throw water at the other and a race would ensue around the house. Maybe they would decide to paint the wall with lipstick or permanent ink markers, oatmeal or Clorox. Maybe they would decide to trim the trees and cut down our 30-foot pine tree. One day they saw the rain starting to fall and decided to put Thompson's water seal on the car to protect it from the rain. Many times they truly tried to do something good but it turned out to be a disaster! I began to respond in anger with harsh words, and in harsh ways.

I was by nature a quiet person; Michael, my husband was also. We loved the quiet. We loved quiet music. We loved quiet thoughts. We loved tranquility and peace. We loved to read in peace. But one of the children had a loud booming voice and it rang throughout the house. Whenever he was awake, there was no more peace. It grated on all of our nerves and caused us to respond to him in frustration a great deal of the time. Who could concentrate on Reading, Algebra, Calculus, Spanish, an end of the term paper or listening to a radio program with all of the verbal clatter and constant motion? I was already getting up in the wee hours of the morning for peace and quiet. But my body was no longer desiring to rise so early any more. It was plum worn out. I would get up as early as I could to accomplish the many needed tasks, but after refereeing arguments and fighting to have a time of prayer in the mornings, I would be depleted of my energy. Since the older children were so understanding and willing to watch the younger boys, there were days when I chose to respond by going back to sleep for a few hours to get replenished.

I was giving too much to others and too little to myself. I was doing too much for the children and for my husband. I was burned out from trying to share the things we learned with others to help them be successful in their home schooling experience, yet I was not receiving encouragement or friendship in return. I did not have the time to invest in friendships. I was burned out from fighting with demons in spiritual warfare. I was burned out because I was beginning to believe the lies from the enemy that nobody loved me, that nobody really cared, that I was all alone, that I had no one to go to and no one who could really understand. I didn't realize it until after my sister committed suicide, that part of my problem might have been depression. Her death in a way saved my life, because it gave me a reason to have to get up and leave the house for her funeral and get out from the chaotic situation in my home. I had to drag myself off of the couch and go.

I didn't realize it until much later, that my ambitions clouded my thinking and blinded me from the blessings already given by God through my husband. I didn't realize that my ambitions drove me to think wrong thoughts. I thought that after his career was over, there would be time for me, a sort of "it's my turn kind of attitude." This took away from my present happiness but it also drove me and gave me a sense of goals. This gave me something to work toward or look forward too.

I didn't realize I was suffering from the sin of perfectionism. It wasn't good enough just to do a thing, it had to be done right! We had to conquer it, master it, and know it! When things began to not go right, I began to feel like this whole home schooling thing was a mess, my marriage was a mess, my children were a mess, and I was a mess. I began to feel that all those years of work, of struggling through home schooling were in vain…I began to believe that this whole picture I had painted in my mind of our Christian family was all ruined. Something in me died. Something in me felt broken. I shared and shared and tried to be transparent but no body seemed to care and even fewer seemed to respond or say anything back to me. This hurt even more. Somehow, somewhere inside of me, I wanted somebody to care about me. I recognized that I was focusing on me but I didn't realize I was suffering from self-centeredness. I had spent 18 years of service to the Lord focusing on others and now I had expectations for the way people were suppose to respond. I had expectations that no person could meet, because it was reserved for God alone.

When you are feeling all burned up and feel that you are a lower than a dust ball. When you feel so small and insignificant and worthless. When your energy is depleted and your mind cannot even think another thought. You are totally burned up. Then is it time to look up. It is time to look into the face of Jesus. It is time to look into His eyes and see your reflection. Imagine the Father as He picks up that handful of dust (you) and breathes life back into it. Imagine His delight in you, His beautiful creation. Imagine His joy at creating you in His image. Imagine His pleasure in forming you as the work of His hands. Imagine how adorned you are with His spiritual gifts as you serve Him as priest in the priest-hood of believers. Imagine how radiant you look all dressed up in purity and in love as His bride- the church. Imagine Him speaking at the conclusion of His work - saying, "It is good! It is good! It is good!"

Now don't you feel lovely? Don't you feel delicate and dainty? Don't you feel loved and cherished? If you don't, go back to the place and reread "Then it is time to look up." Read it and read it again until the truth soaks in your soul. God loves you! Now, you must never again look at your worth in terms of what you did in the past, what you do now, your accomplishments or lack of them. You must never again base your worth on your husband's estimation or your children opinion or what others think. You must "set your mind on things above where your life is now hidden with Christ in God." As a child of God, you have the mind of Christ. As a child of God, He offers you so much!

> # I had expectations that no person could meet, because it was reserved for God alone.

I think too, there are times when God tests our hearts. These are the times when difficulties and testing comes. We can blame God for the trouble or at the very least blame Him for allowing it happen or we can purposely praise Him in the midst of it. He understands our grief and pain like no one else can. We do not have to understand its' purpose, we can rest knowing that He promises to work it all out for our good. Yes, that's easy to say and hard to do, but that is the basis of faith. Faith is that trusting, believing, hoping, knowing that everything is going to work out for the best even when we can't see it with our visible eyes but knowing it in our hearts. As Hebrews 11:1 says, "Faith is being sure of what we hope for and certain of what we do not see."

There is one place in the Bible where we find God allowing Satan to have direct access to a saint. This is in the book of Job. This is the only book of the Bible where we can read a fairly long discourse concerning troubles in the life of a righteous man and read of a conversation between God & Job. God listened to Job then Job listened to God. They communicated. God allowed some circumstances to come into Job's life when he least expected it. Job didn't understand. Job wanted to plead his case before God because he knew the things he had been doing in his worship of God. God allowed trouble to come into Job's life. After it was all over, God blessed the latter half of Job's life more than the first part. God in His sovereignty knew Job's heart long before He allowed Satan to attack. (Job 1:12) He knew that Job was blameless and upright, he feared God and shunned evil" (Job 1:1, 1:8, and 2:3)

During the years of home schooling, God will allow your family to cross many peaks and valleys. He will use the journey to teach you lessons that will prepare you for the kingdom of heaven. It is so wonderful to experience the joy of the mountaintop experiences, but who wants to travel in the sad valleys of life? In the valley, I discovered comfort amongst the broken-hearted as no one else can comfort. I found comfort in young people who had overcome difficulties either by accidents, illnesses or with a sinful past created by themselves or at the hands of others. I found comfort in older people who had lived many different lives and had many different tales to tell. I found comfort amongst the singles or widows who came to understand the word dependence. I found comfort among the elderly or the sick with bodies failing them. I found comfort among those in prison. I found comfort among those once imprisoned by their addictions either sexual, drug or mental. I discovered transparency at the most basic level, and in the rawest state because it is nearly impossible to hide scars, wounds, hurt, trouble or pain forever or when the wound hurts so deeply. It is in the valley that I learned to seek Him more diligently, to desire Him more ferverently, to call out to Him by His names, to walk with Him more confidently in His Sovereignty and in the assurance of His love.

During my days of despair, I simply didn't want to be here on this earth. I wanted to lay my head down on the pillow and go to sleep and never wake up. I just wanted to be relieved from my emotional distresses and from the pain in my heart. I didn't want to commit suicide and hurt my family or my friends. But Satan was throwing every possible option at me in every way imaginable. I recognized him, and I fought him with scripture and prayer but I grew weary.

God knew my need. He was faithful to bring alongside me those who would minister and comfort. He taught me how to encourage others in the valley, by walking with them. He showed me that hurting people need more than just a Bible verse thrown at them or a challenge to rise to the occasion, but they need the human touch of God's love expressed in many ways.

During this time, God also taught me another way to die. He showed me how to give myself away even when I didn't have the physical, emotional or spiritual strength to do it. He taught me the meaning of Paul words "to live is Christ but to die is gain." My purpose and my existence was to be just like Jesus, to "have the same attitude being in very nature God, did not consider equality something to be grasped but taking the very nature of a servant he became obedient to death, even death on a cross." My goal was to be gentle and humble in heart, just like Jesus. My goal was to do the Father's will, just like Jesus. My goal was to seek and save the lost, just like Jesus. My goal was to lift up and encourage the weak, just like Jesus. My goal was to spur my fellow brothers and sisters on toward love and good deeds, just like Jesus. He would determine the time for my departure from this earth.

"I tell you the truth,
Unless a kernel of wheat falls to the ground and dies,
It remains only a single seed.
But if it dies, it produces many seeds.
The man who loves his life will lose it,
While the man who hates his life in this world
Will keep it for eternal life.
Whoever serves me must follow me;
Where I am, my servant also will be.
My father will honor the one who serves me."
John 12:24

"Trust in the Lord with ALL of your heart and lean not in your own understanding, in ALL your ways acknowledge Him and He will make your paths straight…" (Proverbs 3:5,6)

If You're Ever Going To Love Me, Love Me Now

Anonymous

If you're ever going to love me, love me now.

While I can know the sweet and tender feelings,

Which from true affection flow.

Love me now while I am living,

Do not wait until I am gone,

And then have it chiseled in marble,

Sweet words on ice stone.

If you ever have tender thoughts of me,

Please tell me now.

If you wait until I am sleeping,

Never to awaken,

There will be death between us,

And I won't hear you then.

So, if you love me,

Even a little bit,

Let me know while I am living

So I can treasure it.

(Shared by Sharon Thompson)

<h1 style="text-align:center">Chapter 31</h1>

<h1 style="text-align:center">The Love Triangle</h1>

"For God so loved the world, that He
Gave His one and only Son,
That whoever believes in
Him shall not perish
But have
Eternal
Life."
John 3:16

obody loves me! Nobody cares about me! Not my husband! Not my children! Not my friends! Nobody!" I sobbed to my husband on one of the few Saturday mornings that we relaxed in bed. "That's not true!" he said, and he proceeded to list a whole host of examples of how love had been expressed to me in various ways. His statements were true. In my head, I knew they were. God had blessed me with life, a great husband, wonderful children, many friends, a job as mother and a house full of material blessings. Even though I knew he was right, I still didn't "feel" loved. Something inside of me was broken. It was that part of my heart that experienced emotion. In time, I learned that I was suffering from damaged emotions.

"I've tried to explain to you, that I need to hear you communicate verbally. I need to hear you express your thoughts, your feelings, and your emotions to me on a daily basis. When we aren't connected all week long, every day, coming into the weekend feels like I'm trying to communicate with a stranger." As we progressed deeper into our level of communication, I felt freed up to really share. "I think part of the reason I feel this way is because I do not have the trust and security of our relationship that I once had. I use to think one way, but when you betrayed my trust, this spoke volumes to me. It made me feel value-less, worthless. I was working my hardest. I was trying my best to be the best wife that I could at the time considering the circumstances of a traveling husband, struggling learners, maintaining a home and home schooling. I was trying to be the best mother. I was trying to be the best friend to whomever the Lord led across my path. I was in the Word. I was praying. I was serving the Lord." I did not understand…and the more I tried to understand, the worse I felt.

I didn't mean to do it, but it was as if my brain were like a broken record. My song of life would play, but it would continually come back around and get stuck on the same little nick in my record of memories. It was not that I consciously harbored unforgiveness, bitterness or anger. It was a hurt in my heart that ran so deep that I couldn't seem to shake it. Because I could not shake it, I saw it cripple not only my husband, but my children and me as well. It crippled my ministry because I did not feel as happy and free as before. I was physically drained of precious energy. I was mentally tormented by wrong thoughts. I slowly began to close up into my self-centered, pity-partying world. I kept telling myself that nobody loved me. I began to think that God didn't love me either and it wasn't long before I was convinced.

I believed a lie. I was basing my worth on another human being instead of my spiritual position in Christ. Sin (wrong doing) had caused a breech in our relationship with each other and with God. This was only one example of the many love dilemmas we faced in our home schooling adventure. Home schooling for the long haul will require love, much love and a tremendous amount of dedication. For throughout the years of home schooling, love is the glue that holds everything together.

This love triangle chapter has been another one of the hardest chapters to write. It is difficult to try and convey all the aspects of love required in the task of home educating but we believe it is worth an attempt even if it falls short. In our human efforts, we may do a poor job of communicating the descriptions of love as it pertains to home schooling, but we trust God to clarify and make it plain in each family situation.

First of all, we are going to break this love into several categories. One of the first aspects of love, is God's love for us. This involves His decision to send His Son Jesus, as an offering for our sins. It involves His love in the promises of His Holy Spirit, the spirit of truth. He will never leave us nor forsake us. (John 16:5-11) The second aspect of love, is our love for God. This involves our response to Him. We believe Him, we trust Him, we love Him, and therefore we obey Him. This includes the love we have for our spouse and our children. It also includes our decision to home school in obedience to the commands to teach and train our children about Him. The third aspect of love, is the love we have for others outside of our immediate family members. It involves those inside and outside of the body of believers. It is not an act, but a loving response to others because of the Spirit of Christ who resides in the heart of the believer.

God's Love For Us

"How great is the love the Father has lavished on us, that we should be called children of God!" John 3:1

Does God really care about us? If so, how can we know for sure? We've heard it said many times before, "For the Bible tells me so!" But where in today's society which is filled with terrorism, hatred, greed, sexual immorality, lust, anger, and violence, do we see God's love for us? Where in today's society with the break down of the family, the redefinition of male and female, the redefinition of when does life begin, tragedy after tragedy, do we see God's love for us?

In order to answer that question our journey must begin in the book of Genesis, where we find the designer and creator Elohim setting in motion His masterpiece in the establishment of the world and humanity. God set forth the institution of the family. The family is a place where love should abound. The family is a symbolic picture here on earth, which sets the stage for heaven itself. God set forth rules and regulations by which His people were to operate. Not for His good, but for the good of mankind that He created. God knows how He designed His creation and He knows best how His creation is the function. Yet throughout time, we see the continual breaking of His laws and the consequences that followed. God is holy. God is also desirous of a love relationship with His creation. But He cannot tolerate sin in His presence. Sin destroys all that is good. Therefore, there must be a penalty for sin. That penalty could never be paid by the sacrifice of rams and goats, but that penalty was paid in full by the death of Jesus Christ over two thousand years ago. God provided a way for all of mankind to receive His greatest gift. God sent His Son, His one and only Son, Jesus as a substitute for our sins, because of His immense love for mankind.

He loved us enough to create us. He loved us enough to provide a sacrifice for our sins. He loves us still today!

As a member of the human race, each individual is at the center of God's love. He did it all, just for you! He did it all, for every single individual who has been born on the face of this planet. It matters not what religion you claim to be, God loves you!

While God Himself extends an open invitation to experience His love, not everyone will accept this invitation. Sin continues to divide and separate. For the believer (one who acknowledges that Jesus Christ has come in the flesh and confesses with their mouth that God raised him from the dead), there is no sin in this world that can separate him or her from the love of God. (Romans 8:28).

By design, God created the family. As a man and woman leave their fathers and mothers and come together to create a new union, they will establish a home. This home should be a place where the man is the spiritual leader, protector and provider of that home. By design, God created the husband to love his wife (Ephesians 5:25). He is not only to love her, but also to love her as he would his own body. The husband is to love the wife as Christ loved the church. This is a mighty, dynamic, powerful, sacrificial, all-encompassing, enduring, pure kind of love. At the birth of his children, a teaching ministry begins. He is to teach the praiseworthy deeds of the God who created him. He is to represent to these children, his wife, and the world-God the Father.

By design, God created the woman to be the helpmate of her man. He designed her to submit and to respect her husband. He also placed within her a yearning to desire him. (Genesis 3:16). At the birth of their children, she begins a nurturing, caring ministry. Her job is model love and to establish an environment where love is taught and training in righteousness occurs.

In spite of all the possibilities God gave the family to express and receive love, there is no human being on earth that can ever fill the void in the human heart that God placed there to be filled by Himself. Only He and He alone can fill the void the human heart seeks. God (The Spirit of Christ, The Holy Spirit) in us gives us the ability to love. God is the apex of the love triangle.

Our Love For God

"Love the Lord your God with all of your heart and all of your soul and all of your strength. These commandments that I give you are to be upon your hearts. Impress them on your children. Talk about them when you sit at home and when you walk along the road, when you lie down and when you get up."
(Deuteronomy 6:5-8)

When we believe God and love Him, we want to express that love in ways that are pleasing to Him. In our specific case, we believed God, we believed the scriptures and we wanted to express our love for God by teaching our children about Him and His ways. The best way for us to do that, was to home school.

According to the scriptures in both Old and the New Testament, we see examples of various saints' love for God and the tangible expression of that love. Job was one example. Job loved God. In the opening chapter of the Book of Job, we find a devoted man. He is a devoted family man yet also devoted to doing good to those around him. Suddenly, without warning, trouble is thrust upon him. How will he respond?

We find that Job had a love for God and God had a love for Job that carried him through these troubled times. Job's trust in His God, sustained him as he faced several perplexing dilemmas involving the God he served. It was stated that Job had "instructed many, strengthened the feeble, supported those who stumbled, strengthened faltering knees, yet when trouble came upon him, there was nothing he could do." Initially he responded well, but after a time he became discouraged. "Why?" He continually asked himself. "What he had done wrong?" He could not understand. He desired to speak to the Almighty. (Job 13:3) Job loved God. This is why he could say, "Though he slay me, yet will I hope in Him." This is why Job could say, "I will surely defend my ways to his face." (Job 13:15)

In your life? In you homes? In your home schools? Have you gotten to the place where you love God this much? Have you gotten to the place where even if God placed you in the midst of the worse possible trial you could think of, that you would you would still love Him? Well, this is exactly the place where God desires for you to be. He wants you close to His heart. His heart is full of compassion, mercy and grace. He wants you to identify with Christ, His son, our Savior and Lord. He is constantly interceding and praying on our behalf. He is gentle and humble in heart. He wants you to be keenly aware that we truly are surrounded by a great cloud of witnesses who have gone on before you. Many, many people have suffered for the cause of Christ. We are to deny ourselves, take up our crosses and follow Him. In love, He served. In love, we should love. In fact, because I love God: I must read, heed and lead.

1. I must read the instruction manual: The Bible.

2. I must heed the instruction manual. I must have a personal relationship with the Son (Jesus) in order to have a relationship with the Father. I must believe that Jesus Christ is the Son of God. To live the victorious Christian life, I must be empowered by the Holy Spirit. I must present my body as a living sacrifice. I must recognize that I am a soldier in His army. I must set my mind on things above. I must remember that this place is not my home. I must acknowledge His sovereignty and His Lordship in my life.

3. I must lead a godly role model for others to follow. I must tell others about Him (Jesus).

Our Love For Our Spouse

"Wives, submit to your husband as to the Lord. For the husband is the head of the wife as Christ is the head of the church, his body, of which he is the Savior. Now as the church submits to Christ, so also wives should submit to their husbands in everything."
"Husbands love your wives as Christ loved the church and gave Himself up for her to make her holy, cleansing her by the washing with water through the word, and to present her to himself as a radiant church, without stain or wrinkle or any other blemish, but holy and blameless. In this same way, husbands ought to love their wives as their own bodies. He who loves his wife loves himself. After all, no one ever hated his own body, but he feeds and cares for it, just as Christ does the church-for we are members of his body."
(Ephesians 5:22-33)

When we marry our spouse, we usually do so believing we have achieved a deep love and admiration for another human being that is unique to any other couple or any other relationship. As a Christian couple and especially as home schoolers, we believe that we are a team, working together to disciple and train our children toward maturity in Christ.

When we come together in marriage, there is a spiritual union between the man and his wife that forms a triangle. It is a spiritual union with God. It completes the couple. The love triangle, designed by God, is intended to bring the couple into one of the closest unions possible with another human being on earth and with God Himself. The love triangle is a symbolic picture of completion, of wholeness, of fulfillment. When love flows from the man to the woman, it is very obvious. She is radiant and lovely. She is secure, confident, loving, giving and serving. When he is sensitive to her needs, this in turn makes him more desirable to her. When he is sensitive and actively seeks to meet the needs of their children, the needs of their home and those in need, this in turn draws her into a deeper admiration of him.

When the love flows from the woman to the man, she desires to help him in every way she can. She respects him. She submits to him. She desires to see him and their family prosper and to be blessed of the Lord. Their love for God, for each other, for their children and the natural physical chemistry that God placed in the design of His creation will often times culminate in the celebration of marriage. This joyous union brings delight, pleasure, rest and relaxation. This joyous union causes an inner regeneration resulting in new power, energy and love for the couple. While the world calls it sex, before the eyes of God and heaven, it is the celebration of marriage!

> **My love for my husband and my commitment to him were rooted in my obedience to God. My submission to my husband was actually my acknowledgement of the Sovereignty of God, the Lordship of Christ, and my yielding to the Spirit of God in me.**

But there is an enemy to the couple. When there is a violation of the covenant of marriage, this breech can cause trouble. Only obedience to God can restore harmony. When Peter asked Jesus "Lord how many times shall I forgive my brother when he sins against me? Up to seven times?" Jesus answered, "I tell you not seven times, but seventy seven times." Forgiveness restores harmony. In Ephesians 4:26, the scriptures tell us "In your anger, do not sin. Do not let the sun go down while you are still angry, and do not give the devil a foothold." Giving up your right to be angry restores harmony. Repentance, understanding, compassion, patience and a restoration of godly principles in your marriage, will restore harmony.

There were times in Michael and my marriage when God had to show me that my sin was equally as grievous to Him. At times, I was so busy condemning my husband that I did not see my own shortcomings. I had to learn to love my husband unconditionally. I had to learn that my love for my husband was not to be based on feelings but on the fact of the covenant he and I made with God during our wedding vows. We vowed before God Almighty and many witnesses "To love and to cherish, for better or for worse, from this day forward til death do us part...." My love for my husband and my commitment to him were rooted in my obedience to God. My submission to my husband was actually my acknowledgement of the Sovereignty of God, the Lordship of Christ, and my yieldedness to the Spirit of God in me. Whenever I had trouble loving, I learned to recite 1 Corinthians 13 and I put my name in it: Jacqueline is patient, Jacqueline is a kind. She does not envy. She does not boast. She is not rude. She keeps no record of wrong. She rejoices with the truth.... I quickly realized that I feel short of this definition of love, that only God could love this way. But it was to be my standard for living!

Our Love For Our Children

"Be imitators of God, therefore, as dearly loved children, and live a life of love, just as Christ loves us and gave himself up as a fragrant offering and sacrifice to God."
Ephesians (5:1)

When we believe that our children are gifts from God, it makes us want to take care of the gifts. They are not our personal property. They do not belong to us, they are on loan. When we realize that these children are placed in our care for such a short time and are then to be launched into the world for His purposes, it makes us determined to complete our God-given task. One particular day, I was having an especially difficult day with the two younger adopted sons. I was beginning to have all kinds of thoughts ranging from bitter, angry thoughts to thoughts of hopelessness and desperation. They were frustrating me to the max. I was praying and reciting every verse I could think of. When I felt as if I couldn't take it anymore, I verbally cried it out aloud to God. "I can't take it anymore!" and I began to cry. "I thought You didn't give people more than they could handle God, well this is just too much," I told Him again, "this is too much!" as if He were deaf, and I then began to cry.

213

Nothing happened. There was silence. There was no booming thunder. There was no sudden ringing of the telephone. There was no sense of peace. There was nothing! *Where was God throughout this entire struggle?* I wondered. The boys stared at me while they sat on their bar stools at the kitchen counter. I began to reflect and mentally trod the difficult path our family had traveled with their parenting. *Was this my fault? Is this hereditary? Is this learned behavior? Is this some kind of dysfunction of their brains? Is this a manipulation of my kindness? Is this due to maltreatment by siblings?* The more I pondered, the more frustrated and confused I became, because to me the cost had been too much. "It's too much God!" I continued as I washed the dishes and put them away. I was starting to mentally tally up the cost of all the troubles. *The burned barn, the cut-up car seats, the ruined carpets, the painted walls, the torn school books, the ripped clothes, the lost shoes, the broken bikes, the lost tools.... the never ending list kept growing with the remembrance of every trial. Love keeps no records of wrongs*, I thought.

While I sniffled and cleaned the counter, a strange thought entered my mind. I never heard an audible voice, but I heard a quiet question. *How much is a soul worth*? I repeated the question silently in my mind. *How much is a soul worth*? Visions of my Lord with the thorns in his brow came to mind. I could visualize the beads of sweat on his brow. The thought of the nails that pierced his hands and feet melted my anxiety into shame. Suddenly I felt quieted in my anxious state. Nothing in the room changed, except that I became aware of the presence of the Lord. I placed my hand over my mouth and dared not even think another thought. Again, the question resurfaced in my mind, *How much is a soul worth*? I felt so small and ashamed as I realized the price that He had paid was far more than any little insignificant inconvenience we had endured. He led me to the book of Hebrews, "During the days of Jesus' life on earth, he offered up prayers and petitions with loud cries and tears to the one who could save him from death, and he was heard because of his reverent submission. Although he was a son, he learned obedience from what he suffered and once made perfect, he became the source of eternal salvation for all who obey him and was designated by God to be high priest in the order of Melchizedek."

> *How much is a soul worth*? **I repeated the question silently in my mind.** *How much is a soul worth*? **Visions of my Lord with the thorns in his brow came to mind. I could visualize the beads of sweat on his brow. The thought of the nails that pierced his hands and feet melted my anxiety into shame.**

I had to remember that God had children too. He loved and still loves His children. He gave, He blessed, and He did every possible for His children. Yet, His children had broken His heart also. His children had cost him a tremendous amount. If not for His love, which covers a multitude of sins there would be no hope.

Our Love For Others

"This is how we know what love is:
Jesus Christ laid down his life for us.
And we ought to lay down our lives for our brothers.
If anyone has material possessions and sees his brother in need but has no pity on him,
How can the love of God be in him? Dear children, let us not love with words or tongue
But with actions and in truth.
This then is how we know that belong to the truth,
And how we set our hearts at rest in His presence whenever our hearts condemn us.
For God is greater than our hearts, and He knows everything."
I John 3:16-20

Love binds us to an allegiance to God. Love binds us to an allegiance to a husband or wife. Love binds us to an allegiance to their children. Love binds us to an allegiance to serve others. Love will drop off a bag of groceries to a family in need. Love will prepare a meal. Love will visit the sick and shut-ins. Love will write a check. Love will go the extra mile. God in us gives us joy, strength, and the will to love even the unlovely.

Love Is The Key

I Corinthians 13

Love is powerful. "Love is patient, love is kind, it does not envy, it does not boast, it is not rude, it is not easily angered. It keeps no record of wrong." (I Corinthians 13:1-13) Love makes one press on. Love drives one to get up out of a cold bed and go to work to provide. Love will energize and thrust one forward against the seemingly impossible odds. Love will rub a neck or a foot or give a hug. Love will do what need to get done. Love covers a multitude of sins. God is love.

Love Serves

Your Love Is Incomprehensible

By Jacqueline Olivia Cross

I love being in your presence, Lord
I love basking in the warmth of your love
I love feeding on your word, Lord
I love hearing messages from above.

And I know that your love is in-com-pre-hen-si-ble!
Yes, you love me
Yes, you love me.

I love walking in the Spirit, Lord
I love lifting holy hands to you
I love singing praise unto you, Lord
I love being blessed beyond belief.

And I know that your love is in-com-pre-hen-si-ble!
Yes, you love me
Yes, you love me.

I love seeking out your answers, Lord
I love hearing you when you call
I love comfort in my sorrow, Lord
I love knowing you're my all in all

And I know that your love is in-com-pre-hen-si-ble!
Yes, you love me
Yes, you love me.
Yes, you love me
Yes, you love me.

217

Chapter 32

The Climbing Roses

"I am the true vine, and my Father is the gardener.
He cuts off every branch in me that bears no fruit,
While every branch that does bear fruit, He prunes
So that it will be even more fruitful."
John 15:1,2

I am the vine; you are the branches.
If a man remains in me and I in him,
He will bear much fruit;
Apart from me you can do nothing."
John 15:1,2

"Consider it pure joy, my brothers,
Whenever you face trials of many kinds,
Because you know that the testing of your faith develops perseverance."
Perseverance must finish its work so that you may be mature and complete,
Not lacking anything."
James 1:1-4
I am the Rose of Sharon, a lily of the valleys."
Song of Solomon 2:1

I had no sooner walked out of the front door and stepped onto my sidewalk when I looked down to see my once two beautiful climbing rose bushes shriveled and brown. One of the children decided to spray several hundred flies that were resting on the wall of the house with a potent bug spray and "accidentally" nearly killed my two rose bushes. The summer before their growth had been spectacular. There were shoots in several places three and four feet long budding with beautiful dark pink roses. This summer I was expecting those climbing roses to be in their glory full of blooms for me to smell, look at, clip and enjoy.

But, that didn't happen. I had to take the pruning shears to cut off the dead portion of the branches and then lop off one thick branch growing out of control. I was hoping to make the rest of the plant more fruitful. The bush did not speak back in English, but it was obvious that the pruning had negatively affected the plant. It looked stressed. It reminded me of my own situation. It seemed to reflect my feelings and my pain. As I watched the plants for the next several weeks, I was again reminded of the parable of the vine in John 15. I began to see the fruit through the promises God's word offered as I pondered these verses and reflected over my past disappointments. I couldn't see it as I was going through it, but as I looked back now, I could see where God was working all the time and working "all things together for good."

Though hard for us human beings to accept, there is a purpose in pain. God's purpose in pain is always for more fruit. Whether that fruit be in the salvation of souls or in the development of character within an individuals' life. Suffering produces character, it deepens and strengthens faith, it forces us to think beyond the here and now and gives us hope in a future in heaven with God.

Looking back, we can see where God's pruning did produce fruit:

- Our struggle in marriage, led us to becoming closer with each other. We were able to host marriage classes through video in our home for twelve weeks with four other couples.
- Our struggle to know Him better, led to us teaching basic Christianity classes both in our home and in several churches.
- Our struggle to open a resource center, led to establishment of many friendships and a home schoolers co-operative between five families.
- Our struggle to open a resource center, led to a ministry to the elderly at Hillside Retirement Home and a ministry of encouragement to others who came through the doors not associated with home schooling.
- Our struggles led to a ministry to the broken-hearted: the hurting hearts included those with marital problems, financial problems, children problems, victims of rape, incest, eating disorders, physical abuse, verbal abuse and more.
- Our struggles led to a Tuesday night Bible study called <u>Experiencing God</u> by Henry Blackaby to women who held jobs all day.
- Our struggles led to the opportunity for training through Prison Fellowship.
- Our struggles led to an opportunity to lead Bible Study at the MonDay Correctional Facilities in Dayton/Prison Fellowship Training.

- Our struggles led to the writing of a "Witness Booklet" to help others share their faith.

- Our struggles led to the writing of a Marriage Notebook.

- Our struggles led to ministry to the residents of the Hilltop Apartments in Dayton.

- Our struggles led to a deeper understanding of the Sovereignty of God. We were forced to look beyond the circumstances. We were forced to stop blaming God. We were forced to see that natural logical consequences to sin (any wrongdoing against God) can also lead to pruning and thus produce fruit.

"Progress"

Author Unknown

Until I learned to trust, I never learned to pray,

And I did not fully learn to trust

Til sorrows came my way.

Until I felt my weakness, His strength I never knew;

Nor dreamed til I was stricken, that He could see me through.

Who deepest drinks of sorrow drinks deepest too of grace;

He sends the storm so He Himself can be our hiding place.

His heart that seeks our highest good,

Knows well when things annoy;

We would not long for heaven,

If earth held only joy.

Shared by Kathe Bricker from her Daddy's funeral service bulletin 2001

Chapter 33

Praise The Name of Jesus!

"O Lord, our Lord,
How majestic is your name in all the earth!"
Psalm 8:1

"Let the righteous rejoice in the Lord and take refuge in Him; let all the upright in heart praise Him!"

"Through Jesus,
Therefore, let us continually offer to God a sacrifice of praise—
The fruit of lips that confess His Name."
Hebrews 13:15

Mark was home from Fork Union for the summer, and decided to take a college course to place higher in his academic standing. Since he was not driving yet, I had to drive him into town. That particular day as Matthew, Micah and I waited in the car for him to come out, Micah jumped out of the parked car to pick up a little pebble on the sidewalk. He quickly jumped back in and slammed the door. Unbeknownst to me, the window was rolled down about 3 inches and Micah decided to throw the pebble back out. He missed the 3-inch opening and the little pebble hit the car window shattering it into a thousand pieces. Crackling glass fell into the car, out of the car and spilled out onto the sidewalk. My hands gripped the steering wheel while my head slowly fell down to rest on it. "Why Micah? Why? Why did you have to do that?" I asked. "I didn't mean to," he said. I stepped out of the car onto the busy street and went around to assess the damages. Glass was everywhere! I picked up all that I could with my hands and scooped up the rest with an old newspaper.

The next morning I had an appointment at the local glass repair shop. The technician, Mike, came out to the car. He was friendly and I asked if I could sit there while he did the repairs. While he worked, we began to chat. He could tell that I was bummed out about the whole ordeal. We began to talk and share stories. I was extremely encouraged by one bit of advice that he gave me. He had been through some struggles of his own and he gave me his little secret. "Praise!" he said. "You've just got to praise Him when things get tough. That's the way I've made it." He was right. That day, I determined a new course of action, mine would be to praise Him.

God began to move me out of my comfort zone and this required total dependence on Him. He led me to teach working women in evening classes. One evening as Diane & I were co-leading a Bible study called Lord I Want To Know You by Kay Arthur, I brought a globe into the room to illustrate the lesson. This study introduced us to the various names of God. After we read through the lesson, I told the class that I wanted to give them a visual aid for one of the names. I took out a bottle that I had relabeled "LOVE." I unscrewed the cap and began to slowly pour the contents over and around the globe. The red paint that I selected looked so much like blood, that as it rolled and dripped down the sides of the globe, it left a definite impression that words cannot describe on all of our hearts. Here with our eyes, we beheld what "El Shaddai" had done for us. He had poured forth His life's blood for each of us over two thousand years ago. He was a tiny little baby, born to die. One commentator titled the meaning of "El Shaddai" as "the all-sufficient one," another "the God Almighty," yet another, "the pourer forth of His life's blood."

I took out some sticky notes on which I had jotted down some inspired thoughts concerning sin. I wanted to open their eyes to the "Heavenly perspective." I began to ask the ladies if God's grace was sufficient to cover each of the sins I named. One by one I named off every sin I could possibly think of…then I dipped each piece of paper with the known offense into the blood. God's grace was sufficient! His life's blood has covered the sins of the whole world, though not every one will choose to accept His offer of forgiveness.

Praise His Holy Name

I came to the study <u>Lord I Want To Know You</u>, seeking Him because I just didn't sense His presence anymore. I couldn't seem to capture the euphoric feelings of fellowship that He & I once enjoyed. I knew that He had not moved, but I had. Yet I couldn't seem to muster the energy to pick up the pace and try anymore. I had lost the consistency and the dynamic of our times together. But when I began to study and learn His names, these are the truths I learned:

- When I am tempted to ask, "Why was I ever born?" I can look out at the sky, trees, animals, and in the mirror and see the handiwork of Elohim. He who knit me together in my mother's womb will be faithful to complete what He started.

- When I am tempted to wonder, "Where is God? I don't see Him. I don't feel Him. There is El El yon- The Most High God reigning Sovereign and Supreme.

- When trials come and it's hard to understand how a God who sees everything can allow some things to happen like the car accident, the diagnosis of cancer, the wayward child, the adulterous affair, the unexpected divorce, the heart attack, the rape, the baby born with problems, the suicide or the murder. Yet, in the name of El Roi- I can see A God who doesn't miss a thing! "The eyes of the Lord are everywhere keeping watch over the wicked and the good."

- When I have been tempted to think and feel unloved, abandoned, disappointed in my human failures and in the failures of my loved ones, El Shaddai is there saying, "I am sufficient!" I am the God Almighty! I am the pourer forth of my life's blood for you! I love you! I love you! I love you! I can walk out into the world and look up, knowing that His blood has sufficiently covered it all by His grace and mercy.

- When I have been tempted to take control of my own circumstances in life, to put "I" at the center, my desires, my wants, there is Adonai! Only He can be Lord and Master on the throne of my life.

- When I fail to recognize God in the here and now. I discover Jehovah-The Self-Existent One. He is the great "I Am" that never changes. He is the same yesterday, today and forever.

- When I have been tempted to think that I have needs unmet, Jehovah jireh has been there to provide for me at my every point of need.

- When my energy has been depleted, the physical disease appears, or the sickness of my mind or heart are so heavy that I cannot bear it, there is Jehovah rapha-the God who heals. By His stripes we are healed!

- When I am tempted to fear and get bound up in my earthly situation, there is Jehovah nissi-the Lord is my banner. His banner over me is love!

- When I am tempted to feel so alone in this world or so different from everyone else, there is Jehovah-mekoddishkem- the Lord who sanctifies and sets me apart from the world. I am a stranger and an alien here. This place is not my home. I am not supposed to look like the world.

- When I am tempted to see only the chaos, destruction and confusion in this world, there is Jehovah -shalom, bringing peace to my soul. The peace that He gives is the same peace that the world offers.

- When I am tempted to think that the enemy is winning- that wickedness is triumphantly raising it's ugly head, there is Jehovah sabaoth-the Lord of Hosts- He commands a vast army, and the victory is His! He has already won it!

- When I am tempted to think that I am in control. I can look out of my kitchen window and see my sheep. They can't do anything for themselves. I feed them and water them and protect them from harm. We too have a shepherd, Jehovah raah. He is the Lord our shepherd. He shows us where fresh pasture lies to feed us. He guides us to drink of the Living water. He soothes and comforts us with His healing balms. He loves us from the cradle to the grave.

- When I am tempted to think I did something so great for the Lord- He reminds me that my righteousness is as filthy rags. He is my righteousness-Jehovah Tsidkenu.

- When I am tempted to think that I am a teeny, tiny little human being so alone down here on this earth, that God is way up there in heaven, He reminds me that He is Jehovah shammah-the Lord who is there. His presence is in me. The Spirit of God dwells in me. I am never alone. God has been faithful to me! God has been faithful to you! God has been so faithful!

Home schoolers remember to praise Him in all things. As the song goes,

"Praise Him in the morning when you see the sun arising,

Praise Him in the evening cause He took you through the day

And in the in between times when you feel the pressure growing

Remember that He loves you and He promises to stay."

"Rejoice in the Lord always,

Again I say Rejoice!

Philippians 4:4

Chapter 34

The Realities of Home Schooling

"Consider it pure joy, my brothers,
Whenever you face trials of many kinds,
Because you know that the testing of your faith develops perseverance. Perseverance must finish its work so
that you may be mature and complete, not lacking anything."
James 1:1-4

In Loving Memory of:

Nathaniel Blair	Regina Hagedorn	Lisa Halsey
Nov 24, 1989-Jan 16, 1995	Jan 15, 1959-Nov 9, 1998	Oct 21, 2000

One afternoon, five-year-old Nathaniel Blair suddenly cried out in pain and fell to the floor. Unknown to his parents, Brian & Laurie, a main artery ruptured in the heart sac of Nathaniel's heart. Within an hour, he went home to be with the Lord. Mike & Sherry Cwiakala's home schooling plans were altered when Mike lost his job and they were forced to put their children in a local Christian school. Don & Regina Hagedorn decided to home school their eight-year-old daughter Sarah. One morning Regina didn't wake up. She went home to be with the Lord. Another family was moving to another state, shortly before their move, Mommy gave birth to their 7th child for her 7th Caesarean (c-section). It was another move and a new baby, a reality of home schooling.

Gary & Kaye Geist lives were altered when Gary fell off a ladder and was badly injured while they home schooled their eight children. They then faced many difficult challenges that came with the birth of their ninth child Hannah who was born with Down's syndrome. Fred & Gilda had just completed their dream home when a tornado blew through leaving them and the children scattered and literally hanging from trees. Tragedy struck again when Fred lost his job and Gilda miscarried their third child Isaac. Tom & Kim Baird's family life was interrupted when their daughter Katie began having medical problems. Jeff & Lisa Halsey were faced with struggles when Lisa was diagnosed with breast cancer. Lisa lay in a hospital bed for over a year at home. She went home to be with the Lord on Oct. 21, 2000.

Whether you are embarking upon your first year of home schooling or your seventh, it's always good to get the year in proper perspective and be reminded of the realities of home educating. Below are a few of the realities that we've discovered and we're sure you'll discover a few of your own:

- Real life is taking place and it is a vital part of educating your children i.e. illnesses, accidents, births, deaths, moves, job changes, job loss, financial stresses, etc.

- Children home all day provide constant wear and tear on the appliances, furniture, house & car. The constant care of children is physically and mentally exhausting.

- Home educating is just plain hard work. At times, it can be physically, spiritually or emotionally draining.

- There may be deviations from your set plans, you may have to change curriculum choices.

- You may find that your child is not ready for structured academics.

- You may find that your child wants to know far beyond your level of expertise in one or more subject areas.

- You may find your child in more need of character training/development than academics.

- You will learn that proper training takes years.

- You may wonder if you're doing the right thing.

- You have an enemy, Satan, who wants to destroy your efforts, create tension, chaos and introduce confusion in your home.

- Your child may view home schooling differently than you. Your child may view home schooling as restrictive. They may see it as keeping them from doing things they want.

There are other areas, where I must be frank about the reality of home schooling. Your socioeconomic level will affect your home schooling endeavors. For example, the type of job or amount of your income will affect your home schooling in terms of curriculum choices and activity involvement. The number of children you have will affect your home schooling activities. Your age affects home schooling in terms of amount of energy and patience level in dealing with children all day. Your ability to balance your relationship with

God, your marriage, your children, home management, school curriculum and outside activities will be some of the greatest challenges and realities you will face as a home educator. Home education is a way of life. It is a choice. It is a reality!

While these incidents are extremely difficult to face, they have the potential of developing character, in addition to bringing hope and encouragement to others. Home schooling is not a promise from God of an easy life, nor does it mean your family is removed from the trials and tribulations of this world. Allow the realities others' have faced and overcome be a beacon of light and hope to you that God will continue to be faithful during your years home educating. Donna Witek, Yvonne Hesler and their families' lives were changed when their mother's were in separate car accidents. Great changes came to their home schools as they handled their loved ones medical needs and took care of their belongings. Chip & Rene Sutton's lives were changed when their house burned down. They and eight of their eleven children lived in two trailers on the back of their property while their house was rebuilt. John & Tammy's lives were devastated when their son Nicholas was hit by a car. It took months of recuperation. Mick & Barb and Ken & Nancy found themselves in a whirlwind of life changes as their small children were diagnosed with Juvenile diabetes. Later, Ken felt a call to serve in Africa. Ken took a leave of absence for several months from work. He took his family with him to minister in Africa. These are the realities we must face as home educators. They are the faith-building circumstances life brings.

Helpful Tips

- Learn to Prioritize- You will have to decide just how clean does your house have to be before you begin your home school day. Do you really need the Better Homes & Garden look? Or maybe you need to clean up so you can find that curriculum you purchased at the last Curriculum Fair. Do you need to go to every field trip? Do you need to make that craft item, teach that Sunday school class, or coach that basketball team?

- Work toward having a place for everything and putting everything in its place

- Have a plan- Know what the individual needs of your child are. Then plan your curriculum accordingly.

- Learn To Be Flexible- Every day is full of opportunities, challenges, and changes. Don't be so rigid that you cannot adjust.

- Have a teachable spirit- be willing to learn. You'll learn from the curriculum, your child, your successes and your failures.

- Learn not to compare yourself with other moms- it always seems like someone else has it all together and is doing more than you.

- Learn not to compare your child with other children- your child is a unique individual developing at his/her own pace.

- Make time for yourself- Read a good book, take a bath, take a walk, get a hair cut, do something you like to do.

- Make time for your spouse- Remember, he was there before the children so continue to work on your relationship. Plan short, cheap, fun dates at least once a week with an overnighter or weekend alone here and there.

- If a family could afford a maid or a live-in helper at times, this would be helpful. Although depending on someone else long-term, has the potential of taking away from the family's ability to learn to manage their own time and job responsibilities.

- Learn to barter and share needs for services, i.e. shopping, naptime, childcare, etc.

- Learn to recognize the tricks of the enemy, and then respond accordingly, "It is written…"

- Pray continually. Visit your prayer closet for wisdom and guidance.

Andrea Matich, Diane Richardson & Jacqueline working on a project

The Older Women teach the Younger Women

Chapter 35

If I Had It To Do Over Again…

"To all perfection, I see a limit; but Your commands are boundless."
Psalm 119:96
"Teach us to number our days aright, that we may gain a heart of wisdom."
Psalm 90:12

ichael and I were working on a woodworking project as we had done so many times before. We had our own personal names for each other, because we found humor in ourselves during these projects. They sometimes seemed to draw out the worse in us. I called him "Brute Force" because his big strong hands always had to do the hardest part of the job and they sometimes destroyed delicate fine work. He called me "Miss Detail" because I tended to be "quality control" making sure that no defect in workmanship occurred. Sometimes, I too destroyed work but this was by my critical tongue.

As usual, we found ourselves at opposite ends of the spectrum when it came down to the final assessment of our product: The Shelf. "I'm done!" he stated confidently. "No, you're not," I said sweetly, "there's a little nick still on the side of the shelf," I countered. He gave me one of those looks. "I'll do it myself," I said smartly as I tried to sand it down to a more perfect state. After some considerable time, I finally had to relent and let him go on to stain and varnish it because the stubborn little nick refused to come out.

Months later, after the shelf had been prominently placed on the wall in a sitting room, I was admiring its' beauty. I was reminiscing over the hard time I had given Michael about that little defect. Now, as I purposely sought to find it, I could not. And even when I did find it, it seemed so tiny and insignificant from the vantage point at which I now stood. It was then that the Lord convicted my heart concerning my critical spirit with people and things, especially where it concerned home schooling and our children. It was as if He was trying to tell me that while we were so up close and personal, working on this project of training in righteousness, we could see every nick, every fault, and every little defect of their character. He reminded me that when He was finished sanding, staining, varnishing and polishing each person that He created, including me, they would be a work of art. Oh! what a thing of beauty His work would be to behold!

Now we know that it is impossible to go back and redo some of our mistakes. It does no good to go back and dwell on our failures and make ourselves sick with guilty consciences. But our purpose in sharing "if I had to do it over again" is our effort for you to be able to learn from our mistakes and for us to give insightful encouragement on ways your family might want to consider making changes—today—to improve your home school experience!

1. If I had it to do over again, I would seek to enjoy each child more as His creation rather than trying to mold or control their behavior.

2. I would relax more. There is a lot of time during the children's growing up years.

3. I would eliminate the "fear" factor. The fear of Child Protective Services coming in to remove my children or the fear of testing or the fear of failing at teaching academics. This "fear" created anxiety in me that produced anger at times directed toward the children or my husband.

4. I would operate more as a husband/wife team. It's not that we didn't, but I tended to be the one attending the home schooling seminars and I thought I was the expert.

5. I would develop a plan to work on character training/manners/social graces before academics.

6. I would concentrate on basic phonics and basic math initially rather than trying to do 6 to 7 subjects per day.

7. I would plan weekly dates with my husband to get away and be a couple. I would use this time to talk through troubling issues & resolve them.

8. I would not adopt children on an emotional whim, as a romanticized notion or as a good deed to society. I would adopt only as a direct leading from God to both spouses and all of the siblings.

9. I would seek help when needed, whether in the area of spiritual, emotional, mental or academics.

10. I would laugh more. I would play more games even though we played quite a bit together as a family.

11. I would pay children for jobs that I wanted to teach lessons about finances, delegating or even how quickly money can be wasted.

12. I would not worry so much but enter home schooling with much more confidence.

13. I would have more children.

14. Early on, I would train more thoroughly in spiritual disciplines.

15. I would teach them how to defend their faith.

16. I would sing more. I would be happier.

17. I would share more openly my own weaknesses. I would be more real.

18. I would take early signs of rebellion/deceit more seriously.

19. I would pay special attention to the attitude of male superiority between the ages of 10-12.

20. I would have the issue of courtship vs. dating settled between the ages of 6-12. There is no purpose in the American system of dating.

21. I would live my life in chapters.

22. I would insist that the father be more involved.

23. I would deal with my own lack of self-control as sin.

24. I would set limits on outside activities and limit commitments.

25. I wouldn't try to make things so fair and even but allow performance/behavior/maturity level determine rewards.

26. I would not send a child to college early.

27. I would pray without ceasing!

28. I would persevere

29. I would more diligently seek to respect and love my wife/husband

30. I would ambitiously seek to nurture, care for and love our children

31. I would remember that we as parents are the experts!

32. I would use the lessons God teaches us to teach the children

33. I would seek to have a teachable spirit!

34. I would seek to learn from our children

35. I would not compare myself with other home schoolers!

36. I would not expect perfectionism, not in your husband, yourself, your children or your home

37. I would have more fun! I would enjoy each other. I would fail, learn, and grow together!

38. I would seek to remember that home schooling is a life style.

39. I would seek to remember that home schooling is a parents' choice and a parents' right.

40. I would not forget that home schooling is challenging but worthwhile!

*Used By Permission of Mrs. Jessie Wise

Closing

"He who began a good work in you will be faithful to complete it."
Philippians 1:6
"Behold! I am coming soon!
My reward is with me and I will give to everyone according to what he has done.
I am the Alpha and the Omega,
The First and the Last,
The beginning and the End."

Revelation 22:12,13

I sat down in the brown recliner in our living room. The sun was beaming through the dirty windows. I had my Bible, my note cards for the ladies Bible study, my pens and my <u>Abiding in Christ</u> devotional reading. "Please Lord let him sleep! I softly mumbled, please give me a little more quiet time before he wakes up." Nine-year-old hyperactive Micah was sound asleep upstairs.

As I sat enjoying the quiet, the constant tick, tick, ticking of the clock became even more prominent. I glanced up to the top of the wall unit. I smiled. I had purposely set up a little scene there the year before as a daily reminder for me "to set my mind on things above." The green clock was to remind me of how important each second is and how time is not to be wasted. I found a decorative gold painted wire throne and three angels at a local store. The throne reminds me that God the Father is seated on that throne-today! Next to the throne is an angel playing a harp to remind me of the beautiful music playing in heaven-today! I can almost the living creatures as "day and night" they never stop saying, "Holy, holy, holy is the Lord God Almighty, who was and is and is to come." Beside the throne is a figure of a lamb given to me by my sister-in-love Jacqueline Anne. This figurine reminds me of the Lamb who is worthy to receive glory, honor and praise. A lone wine glass reminds me of the blood Yeshua/Jesus the Lamb of God shed for me and for the whole world. Next to the lamb is a figurine of praying hands. It is actually a music box that rotates and plays "Amazing Grace." That song is my mother's favorite hymn. The praying hands belonged to my sister

Sheila before her untimely death. It reminds me that Jesus is always praying for me and for those He loves. Tucked in this grouping is a heart-shaped crystal dish containing potpourri. It reminds me of the crystal sea and of the prayers of the saints, being kept in heaven. Two more angels stand out in front poised with their trumpets in midair. I long to hear that trumpet sound and to rise to meet my Lord and Master, my Adonai, my Jesus. Another figurine given to me by my friend Terri of the lion and the lamb lying down together, remind me of our future hope, a new heaven and a new earth. There will be no more pain, no more tears, and no more sorrow. Now the ticking of the clock combined with the quiet got me to reminiscing. *These years of home schooling have been so full. We have worked so hard! We have done so much! We had been so blessed! God has been faithful!*

Today, Michael, my husband is entrenched in his work with Ball Aerospace, but he always finds time for his wife and children. Michael Christopher has been in Texas for three years now. He is working, going to school and involved in ministry with his Uncle Charles. Mark Anthony left the Academy and is back home going to college. Jennifer and Janet are students at Wright State University. They completed two years at Sinclair Community College and graduated from our home school

As I looked around the room, almost everything was neatly in its place. I thought to myself, *this is the way it could have been for the last twenty years. We could have sent them off to school and this house would have been quiet and everything would have stayed in its' place. But then, we would have missed so much!* I looked around the walls at some of our pictures jammed full of our many home schooling adventures. We have accomplished much. We had grown in our relationships and gleaned a lifetime of memories during our years of home educating.

As the war with Iraq looms, the bombs are dropping in Afghanistan, the clean-up of the World Trade Center and broken lives continues in New York, Americans are plagued with the fear of Anthrax or some other unknown germ warfare attack, Michael and I are confident that we have to the best of our ability, with the knowledge we had at the time, we raised our children to be God honoring, law-abiding, intelligent individuals who would be willing to sacrifice of themselves in whatever manner the Lord calls them. We trained them to serve. We did our very best.

Every home schooling family we met was different. They came from different backgrounds. They had different occupations. They were dealing with different situations. They had different religious beliefs. They had different beliefs about raising a family based upon their upbringing and experiences. The people that we met, were all at various levels of spiritually in their Christian walks. They were all unique! But even in those differences, some things were common to us all. One was the fact that God had created us male and female. Second, somehow God with His powerful love had drawn us together as a couple and together we had brought forth these children whether by birth, remarriage or adoption. Third, we saw the love parents had for their children and the desire for their well-being. Fourth, most parents recognized the fact that these children were gifts from the Lord, divinely endowed with gifting of their own. Fifth, we saw families as a symbolic picture of the body of Christ. Sixth, we saw the critical need for fellowship amongst believing families in their community. Seventh, we saw how families made up a divine team here on earth and if they will live according to the scriptures throughout their lifetime, they will discover their powerful influence upon their world.

The scriptures tell us "without faith it is impossible to please God." (Hebrews 11:6) Home schooling is very much a faith walk. Like Abraham, you will be called to go to a place (the unknown territory of life) where you will later receive your inheritance, "the city with foundations, whose architect and builder is God." Like Noah, you are being called to build an ark of protection for your family during this wicked and depraved generation. Like Moses' parents, who saw they had no ordinary child and went against the grain of society, you too will take your place in the annuls of the faithful. Like the prostitute Rahab, who knew she had made mistakes in her lifetime but now wanted to take her stand for righteousness on the side of God, you too will reposition yourself and your family.

> *"Training in godliness takes time. It is daily yielding your will to His. It is daily submitting. It is daily searching. It is sometimes failing but always getting back up."*

The Bible is foundational to all of life. It is not a decorative book to simply display in the home. It is not a religious book full of laws, rules and regulations for you to grimace through. It is not a book to be read by happenstance with a verse here or there. It is an extremely practical book with teachings for daily living. It is foundational to every discipline known to man: to science, chemistry, biology, astronomy, psychology, sociology, economics, engineering, history, philosophy, mathematics and every other discipline. The Bible is a love letter from God Himself.

Remember, at the beginning of this book when I said "I desired for some older, more experienced woman to take me under her wings and teach me, but I never found her." Well, God revealed to me that He had provided her many times over. Not in one woman, but in several. The first was my own dear mother, Lillian Olivia Stinnett Ware. She is my hero. She has never received all of the letters of commendations that I have written her, thanking her or praising her because they were written in my head during the busy times of raising children. I could cry when I reflect back over the years just thinking of her hard work when I was a child and even today. She modeled for me all of my forty plus years on this earth, the example of a faithful wife, devoted mother and a cherished friend. After raising her own ten children, she went out and worked at Shearer Hills Baptist church for fifteen years with the Mother's Day out program, taking care of "the little children." Today she continues to serve her Lord by serving her children, grandchildren and others. He provided my Mother-In-Love, Audrey Cross. She is both Michael and my mother. I love her so much! She has taught me much about determination, perseverance, laughing and giving. I am thankful for her teaching me how to prepare different Jamaican delicacies. She has truly walked beside us during the twenty-four years of our marriage to encourage us and help us on our way.

My own dear sisters, Carol Carpenter, Glenda Young, Phyllis George-Harrison, deceased sister Sheila Bell and Cheryl Butler have also played their parts in blessing us. Often it was not always in what they said but what they modeled in their lives. And of course, my sisters'-in-love, Miss Jacqueline Anne Cross, Delia George, Eula Ware, and Karen Ware.

Some were sisters in the Lord, neighbors, friends or fellow home schoolers like Kathy Anderson, Diane Allnutt, Maria Berry, Edna (Harris) Booker, Susan (Lembright)Borm,

Sandy Boyette, Kathe Bricker, Jeri Carson, Cindy Campbell, Rhonda Chambers, Ruby Clarke, Nancy Cook, Diane Cope, Mara Curran, Sue Cutting, Barb Denen, Ann Evans, Andi Fisher, Laurie Flowers, Nancy French, Kaye Geist, Gloria Hacker, Laura Hambrick, Ruby Hambrick, Carol Harlow, Cindy Heflin, Joyce Hill, LeAnn Hill, Florence Hoyd, Nancy McGreer, Kris Keese, Yvonne Kress, Meta Law, Judy Legro, Pam Littleton, Gina Miller, Janet Morrin, Merry Moses, Tammy Norcauker, Jo Ann Peters, Jackie Perseghetti, Libby Pidgeon, Sue Ressler, Diane Richardson, Michelle Roebuck, Jeannie Roeck, Mary Sellers, Ginger Smith, Sherry Snell, Jan Soto, Elizabeth Sprague, Betty Springer, Karen Stokes, Rene Sutton, Susan Swedlund, Hiroko Thacker, Sharon Thompson, Karen Tucker, Linda Ulmer, Gloria Van Camp, Tina Vanlandeghem, Glenda West, Debbie Wills, Liz Wilson, Gilda Winkler, and Waynette Young.

Then there were the women who influenced me by radio or their books like Kaye Arthur, Emilie Barnes (also by seminars and friendship), Elizabeth Elliot, Sue Gregg, Cynthia Heald, Grace Ketterman, Beverly LaHaye, Joyce Landorf, Martha Peace, Jo Anne Wallace, Susan Volkhardt and Mimi Wilson.

This book was written for the purpose of serving your family. We believe in you and the plans God has for your family. We deeply want you to succeed at home schooling! This book was written to give you hope and encouragement from beginning to end. God's world was our classroom. It is yours also. In God's strength, you can do it! You can home school successfully!

This may be the end of the writing of this book, but our family continues to fail, learn, and grow. It has been our desire to share a small inkling of our triumphs and trials, our ups and downs in order that you might see a process. A very long process that spans a lifetime and we are not done yet. Training in godliness takes time. It is daily yielding your will to His. It is daily submitting. It is daily searching. It is sometimes failing but always getting back up. It is daily studying His Word to "Show yourself approved as a workman who does not need to be ashamed but who correctly handles the Word of Truth." It is this line upon line and precept upon precept that God grows us to maturity in Christ. It is daily spending time with Him that we learn to abide in Christ, to walk in the Spirit and to accomplish the Father's will her on earth. "Love the Lord your God will all of your heart and all of your soul and all of your mind and the second is like unto it, love your neighbor as your self and you will fulfill all the laws and the prophets…" May God bless you with His everlasting love…

The Cross Family

Critics/Suggestions

In an attempt to share our family's experiences, this writer may have miscommunicated some message. Or maybe the reader may have misunderstood. I believe scripture when it says "accept criticism, get all the help you can." So I invite you to share your thoughts, as long as they follow the Biblical criteria of benefiting those who listen. Thanks for reading! May God bless you!

_____

_____

_____

_____

Critics/Suggestions

In an attempt to share our family's experiences, this writer may have miscommunicated some message. Or maybe the reader may have misunderstood. I believe scripture when it says "accept criticism, get all the help you can." So I invite you to share your thoughts, as long as they follow the Biblical criteria of benefiting those who listen. Thanks for reading! May God bless you!

_____

_____

_____

_____

Order Form

Name _____

Address _____

State _____ Zip _____

Phone Number _____ E-Mail_____

Name to be printed on the front of booklet:

_____

Your testimony should include:

- Description of your life before Christ

- Description of how you came to know Christ

- Description of your life in Christ today

To order, send form, along with your testimony, plus ($5 donation) per booklet to:

Crosspointe Ministries
2435 Anderson Road
Xenia, OH 45385

Order Form

Name _____

Address _____

State _____ Zip _____

Phone Number _____ E-Mail_____

Name to be printed on the front of booklet:

_____

Your testimony should include:

- Description of your life before Christ

- Description of how you came to know Christ

- Description of your life in Christ today

To order, send form, along with your testimony, plus ($5 donation) per booklet to:

Crosspointe Ministries
2435 Anderson Road
Xenia, OH 45385

Your testimony should include:

- **Description of your life before Christ**

_____

_____

_____

_____

_____

_____

- **Description of how you came to know Christ**

_____

_____

_____

_____

_____

_____

- **Description of your life in Christ today**

_____

_____

_____

_____

_____

_____

Suggested Reading List

The books on this Suggested Reading List were extremely helpful and beneficial to our family. I do hope and pray you will *make the time* to read them.

Chapters

The Basic Steps to Successful Home Schooling, Vicki A. Brady, Vital Issue Press,1996
The Peanut Butter Home School Family, Bill Butterworth, Fleming Revell Co., 1987
Home Grown Kids, Dr. Raymond Moore, Word Book Publishers, 1981
Home Spun Schools, Dr. Raymond Moore, Word Book Publishers, 1982
Will Early Education Ruin Your Child?, J. Richard Fugate, Aletheia Division, 1990
Successful Home Schooling, Richard Fugate, Aletheia Press, 1990
The Christian Home School, Gregg Harris, Wolgemuth & Hyatt Publishers Inc., 1988
Basic Child Training, Richard Fugate, Aletheia Division, 1990
Going To School in 1776, John Loeper, Macmillan Publishing Co., 1973
Going To School in 1886, John Loeper, Macmillian Publishing Co., 1984
Training For Royalty
*As you read different home school books and their conflicting philosophies, you must continue to read your Bible so that God will grace you with wisdom to develop your own family's home school philosophy.

What is Schoolproofing?, Mary Pride, Crossway Books, 1988
The Basic Steps to Successful Home Schooling, Vicki A. Brady, Vital Issues Press,1996
Basic Child Training, Richard Fugate, Aletheia Division,
Child Training and the Home School, Jeff & Marge Barth, Parable Publishing, 1991
A Biblical Psychology of Learning, Ruth Beechick, Accent Publishers, Inc., 1982
A Christian Philosophy of Education, Gordon H. Clark, The Trinity Foundation, 1988
Is Public Education Necessary?, Samuel L. Blumenfield, The Paradigm Company, 1985

You Can Home School Successfully, Ruth Beechick, Arrow Press, 1988
Parents Are Teachers Too, Claudia Jones, Williamson Publishing, 1993

The Way They Learn, Cynthia Tobias, Focus on the Family, 1994
Building Character, Gary Mauldaner, Plain Path Publishers, 1988

The Bible Time Nursery Rhyme Book
Teaching Your Child About God, Wes Haystead, Regal Books, 1974
The One Year Book of Devotions for Kids, Children's' Bible Hour, Tyndale House Publisher's, 1993

Discipleship: The Secret To Well Behaved Children-continued
The Master Plan, Win Arn & Charles Arn, Church Growth Press, 1982

About the Author

Jacqueline Olivia Cross was born in San Antonio, Texas on June 11th, 1956 to Charles & Lillian Ware. She was the first born of their seven children. Due to her parents' previous marriages, she grew up as the middle child of twelve other siblings. She attended Cuney Elementary in San Antonio. After a move to Corpus Christi, Texas, she attended Ella Barnes and Martin Junior High. She graduated from Foy H. Moody High School in 1974. She also attended Del Mar Community College.

She served in the United States Air Force from 1975-1979. She was selected as one of the first women airman to attend an all-male institution, The United States Air Force Academy Prep School in 1975. She graduated in May of 1976 and entered The United States Air Force Academy with the first class of women.

Her career as wife and mother span from 1978-to this current year. After an introduction to home schooling by friends in 1982, she and her husband Michael have taught their six children at home. Her love of learning coupled with her love of people has thrust her and her family into one adventure after another. She has been a Support Group Leader, a Sunday school teacher, a soccer coach, a shepherdess, a mentor, a Women's Bible study leader and a friend to many. She is a sheep lover and mothers any creature that comes along.

She deserves a Ph.D. (Professional Home Degree) from Sunrise Christian Academy (the name of their home school) for exemplary service from 1980-2002. She received a Bachelor's degree in Church Ministries with a minor in Educational ministries from Liberty University in 1993 (while home schooling).

She currently is in full time ministry to her husband Michael Anthony Cross. Ball Aerospace in Dayton, Ohio employs him. Her six children Michael, Mark, Jennifer, Janet, Matthew and Micah Cross are her the joy and burden of her heart. They reside on a small five-acre mini-farm in Xenia, Ohio.

She has a passion for doing God's will. Her heart and ministry begins with her family and extends to whomever the Lord leads across her path. Her gracious hospitality has lifted the burden from many a hurting heart. Her tender spot is to mentor and disciple the new believer. Her ministry of encouragement and passion to see the Body of Christ wake-up to the treasure He (God) offers is what she lives for: the fruit.